T0247081

Faith: A Very Short Introduction

VERY SHORT INTRODUCTIONS are for anyone wanting a stimulating and accessible way into a new subject. They are written by experts, and have been translated into more than 45 different languages.

The series began in 1995, and now covers a wide variety of topics in every discipline. The VSI library currently contains over 750 volumes—a Very Short Introduction to everything from Psychology and Philosophy of Science to American History and Relativity—and continues to grow in every subject area.

Very Short Introductions available now:

1

Available soon:

For more information visit our website

www.oup.com/vsi/

Roger Trigg

FAITH

A Very Short Introduction

OXFORD
UNIVERSITY PRESS

Great Clarendon Street, Oxford, OX2 6DP,
United Kingdom

Oxford University Press is a department of the University of Oxford.
It furthers the University's objective of excellence in research, scholarship,
and education by publishing worldwide. Oxford is a registered trade mark of
Oxford University Press in the UK and in certain other countries

Published in the United States of America by Oxford University Press
198 Madison Avenue, New York, NY 10016, United States of America

British Library Cataloguing in Publication Data
Data available

Library of Congress Control Number: 2023951525

ISBN 978-0-19-284926-7

Printed and bound by
CPI Group (UK) Ltd, Croydon, CR0 4YY

MIX
Paper | Supporting
responsible forestry
FSC® C013604

Contents

Preface: The nature of faith

What do we mean by 'faith'? The word is ubiquitous. We hear of 'faith communities', 'faith-based organizations', as well as the faith of individuals. Some may claim that they got through a bad experience because of their faith. These references suggest that 'faith' is a normal synonym for a religious outlook, but the word 'faith' has a resonance beyond religious contexts. Someone could have faith in their doctor, and then the word just suggests trust. The object of our faith could be a person (even God), so that faith is bound up with a relationship, or purely intellectual when I have faith that something is true, and then it seems more like hope.

Sometimes faith is the badge of a community or organization, and at others an individual matter. The faith I was brought up in may not now be my personal faith. The common drift between various senses of what 'faith' can mean even in an avowedly religious context is illustrated by what King Charles III said in Buckingham Palace on his accession to the British throne in 2022 to the leaders of different religions in the United Kingdom, significantly called 'faith leaders'. He has the official title of 'Defender of the Faith' (*Fidei Defensor*), abbreviated as F.D., on all British coins. It was a title conferred in the 16th century, referring specifically to Christian faith. The King was anxious also to stress that he wanted 'to protect the diversity of our country by protecting the space for faith itself, and its practice, through the religions, cultures, traditions and beliefs, to which our hearts and minds direct us as individuals'. He went on to refer to 'my own faith' and his 'membership of the Church of England'. Thus faith, it seems, can at the same time refer to the beliefs of particular religions, even a specific section of one, while also being a generic term for religious belief in general, and even perhaps to wider forms of belief. At the same time, the word 'faith' can refer to both an agreed body of belief, a tradition, held by many people, or the individual commitment of one person.

Philosophical and social pressures make us waver between these various understandings. One dilemma is whether faith, individual or collective, is directed at something beyond itself, or just tells us about the people who express that faith. A similar issue is whether faith is a matter of intellectual belief, or indissolubly linked to action. The connection between beliefs and behaviour, faith and 'works', is important. Modern thought has not just used the blanket term 'faith' to cover many kinds of religion, it has also sometimes used it in a derogatory fashion, putting it beyond the scope of public reasoning. This mode of thinking has gained strength in societies in which there are now many competing religions. It is tempting to assume that, in the face of a cacophony of claims, they are all false. People turn to science, in the quest for certainty, sometimes failing to appreciate how tentative and provisional the findings of science are, given the limitations of human knowledge.

The word 'faith' has a resonance in Christian theology that it does not possess even in the two other great monotheistic religions of Judaism and Islam. It is a word (in Greek *pistis*) constantly used in the New Testament, and throughout Christian theology. An emphasis on it helped St Paul and others to stress a major difference between Christian commitment and the law-based strictures of Judaism. Faith was also understood as reaching out beyond secure knowledge. This is underlined in the Letter to the Hebrews, where the writer defines it as 'the undergirding' or support of 'things that I hope for, and the trial (testing) of what is not seen'. Not surprisingly this has irritated many thinkers, particularly in the modern age, who would like to depend on the certain and secure knowledge that they imagine can be given by science. The relation between faith and reason has inevitably been a constant preoccupation over the last 2,000 years. In more modern times, the idea of individuals being put right before God by their personal faith was championed in the Reformation of the 16th century. Notions of 'justification by faith' caused great social disruption in the major split between Protestantism and Catholicism. The European Enlightenment, starting in the 17th century, originally saw reason, like faith, as a gift from the God who had made humans in his own image. That provided a stimulus for the development of modern empirical science, by people such as Isaac Newton. The French Revolution in the 18th century, however, deified 'Reason', as a rival to the traditional religious faith that it had come to despise.

Nowadays religious faith is again involved in political battles. While many say it is of private concern only, others believe that faith is of universal importance, perhaps even with political implications. They want to be able to practise and express their faith in the public sphere. This has produced cultural clashes in many Western countries. The fact that religious faith typically invokes an authority beyond the reach of the State, or even fashionable public opinion, can threaten any secular State and its way of doing things.

Faith cannot be confined to the home, or even church, mosque, synagogue, or temple. Its holders think they have insights into what is important in human life, and the common good of humans living together. Its existence challenges many societies, particularly those with totalitarian governments. It can also seem a threat to democratic societies. The problem is whether they too can allow their citizens to look to another allegiance beyond the State. The manifestation of different forms of religious faith, and their suppression, can be the source of social division. Without the application of reason, such disputes can only be settled by means of the exercise of arbitrary power. Many think that religious faith is impervious to rational discussion.

The easy assimilation of the idea of faith with that of religion in general carries dangers. A perennial problem of Western scholars trying to understand different societies and religions is the temptation to impose the categories of their own society on others. Unless we fall into the trap of a self-defeating relativism, which restricts us to our own self-contained societies, we must assume that some mutual understanding across cultures and languages is possible. We should, for instance, accept that humans share a common nature and face the same objective world with the same basic problems, although even those two assumptions are challenged in the present age. That does not mean that we can assume that other cultures are just like ours and alternative beliefs will reflect our presuppositions. We must be wary of thinking that other religions, or 'faiths', can be understood on the model of Christianity. An example often quoted has been a tendency to see so-called 'Hinduism' as a single discrete religion on the model of Christianity. The concept of faith itself can be very slippery. It has been so anchored in Christianity, and so central to Christian theology, that it can be misleading to apply the term with all its Christian overtones to other religions in ways they may not find congenial or appropriate. Forcing other religions into a straitjacket constructed by Christian understandings does not do justice to their own character. To group 'faiths' together as somehow similar can lazily assume that, say, Jewish 'faith' is the same as Islamic 'faith', and both are equivalent to its role within Christianity. They may share some basic similarities in believing in one God as Creator of the Universe, and in repudiating the naturalist idea that the physical world is all that there is. Even so, the word 'faith' in Western society is so permeated with Christian theological understandings, and distinctions that we will not easily understand other religions through the prism of the concept. While much of what is said in this book will be relevant to other religions besides Christianity, there can be no escaping the centrality of Christian thinking for understanding the concept, even at the present day.

This becomes more obvious when we look at the origins of the Christian language of faith in the world of the early Roman Empire. At that time, both Greek in the eastern half of the Empire, and Latin in the western half, had words for 'faith'. The Greek word *pistis* and its cognates are used repeatedly in the New Testament. Its original meaning in the ancient world was very similar to the resonances of *fides* in Latin. Both carried with them ideas of virtuous trust, loyalty, reliability, and 'fidelity', essential to individual and communal relationships. Within Christianity, the idea of faith came to play a more expansive (and key) role. References to *pistis* and its cognates in the New Testament far outnumber even those to such foundational concepts as love, salvation, or hope. As one modern classical scholar, Teresa Morgan, puts it at the beginning of a scholarly survey of the ancient notions of *pistis* and *fides*, such concepts play a far less significant role in either Judaism or Graeco-Roman religion than in Christianity. She says: 'The language of faith is central to Christianity as in no other religious tradition: without it, it is impossible to do justice to Christian understandings of the relationship between God and humanity'. At an early point, though not in the New Testament, the new movement became known simply as *he pistis* (the faith), and its adherents as 'the faithful'. With such a background, stretching back nearly two millennia, stripping religious 'faith' of its Christian assumptions will always be challenging.

Acknowledgements

The philosophy of religion is now a flourishing discipline in many countries. The British Society for Philosophy of Religion grew out of a more informal discussion group meeting annually in Oxford, and I was privileged to be its Founding President in 1993. I learnt much from the meetings of the Society and its predecessor, and I am grateful for the many stimulating discussions I have had over many years. The Society is a supporter of the European Society for Philosophy of Religion, of which I have also been President. I am grateful to the contacts I have had through that with philosophers and theologians from many countries across Europe and beyond.

I also owe a personal debt of gratitude to my wife, Julia, for her constant encouragement, and my daughter, Dr Alison Teply, who has helped me with many of the issues raised in this book.

Chapter 1
Faith and reason

Faith and belief

What role have beliefs in any expression of faith? Is 'faith' just a mysterious part of someone's personality, or is it connected with beliefs about what is the case? My faith in my doctor's ability to cure me is misplaced if he or she has, without my knowledge, just been killed in an accident. Even if the doctor is alive but has false qualifications, my faith may be ungrounded, since my beliefs are mistaken. An engineer designing a new suspension bridge can have absolute faith in its specifications, and its ability to withstand high winds. If, though, once built, the structure sways uncontrollably in a storm and breaks up, the engineer's faith has proved to be misplaced.

A typical focus of faith in everyday contexts away from religion involves faith in something or somebody, or faith that something is the case. Such faith is not a magical ingredient that is totally undirected. It is not something you either have or do not have, but has a content that should be rationally examined. You must have some understanding of what or whom you are putting your faith or trust in. Faith is never free-floating, and self-sufficient, but is directed in a particular direction. What is it about? The object of my faith, what I have in mind when I put my trust in something or somebody, must be worthy of my reliance. It must measure up to what my beliefs suggest. Genuine faith purports to be warranted, about a real object, not an imaginary or illusory one.

Faith has its place in ordinary life and is normally associated with beliefs. As with many mental descriptions, beliefs express our orientation to the world, but never imply infallibility. What we think, individually or collectively, about reality, does not always reflect the way the world is. I can be certain it is not going to rain but may still get wet. When nearly everyone believed the earth was flat, that did not make it any less round. A belief in ghosts is no proof of their existence. This mismatch between the contents of the human mind and reality can often be very striking. When it is too great, it can be a sign of mental illness.

The content of beliefs may describe the character of a faith, but not authenticate it. That applies to religious faith, which must also involve claims to truth about something or somebody independent of the believer. It is easy to say that there are no truths, only opinions or beliefs, each of which is as good as any other. Our attention is then transferred from what is true, or we think is true, to the fact that we, or others, believe it. Beliefs become entirely a fact about the individual or group holding them, such as believers of a particular religion. Descriptions of faith then serve as ways of identifying who people are, not the objects of their belief. 'Identity politics' thrives on the idea of competition between different groups, perhaps with different faiths, rather than any idea of a dialogue between different ideas of what reality might be like. When the goal of truth recedes, the issue is not which claims might be right, but who can implement what they want. Coercion of different kinds, rather than dialogue and rational persuasion, is all that is left.

The exact relationship of faith and belief is contested in some contemporary philosophy. This is not only because of a science-based contempt for claims to truth that lie beyond empirical investigation. That can be very prevalent. Another current is more in tune with the pragmatist philosophy of such American thinkers of previous generations as William James and John Dewey. For more than a century, that way of thinking has stressed that action is more salient than abstract speculation. Pragmatist philosophy is typically 'down-to-earth', asking what difference a belief makes to people's lives, and 'cashing out' its meaning in terms of its influence on the way of life. A contemporary philosopher of religion, Jonathan Kvanvig, talking of faith, says that 'such an approach begins at the functional level, characterising the role that faith plays in the lives of people of faith'. Beliefs become secondary and do not define faith. In fact, he considers the same forms of behaviour, such as actions of selfless love, can accompany many different forms of belief in different religions. For him, behaviour, rather than belief, defines faith. That view makes it easier to see similarities between religions, and also downplays the importance of doctrinal disagreement within a single religion.

There are attractions in this position. We can pursue different ideals but behave in similar ways. Faith lies in the pattern of life, rather than in fulfilling intellectual requirements. For Kvanvig, 'faith matters because it involves the setting one's heart on things that matter'. We are still left with the question as to what does really matter. We can admire a person's commitment to a particular way of life and their devotion to it, but may still wonder whether their loyalties are properly directed and whether they are supporting a cause that in reality is worth fighting for. Single-minded faithfulness to any cause may be impressive, but history is littered with examples of the terrible destruction and horror such devotion can bring. Desires and motivations should be well grounded. Faith has traditionally been regarded as a virtue, particularly in a Christian context, but that implies that it is linked with basic moral concerns about truth and goodness. The object of religious faith is assumed to be good. Without that presupposition, wholehearted commitment and faith may even be dangerous. A faithful Nazi might be more threatening than a half-hearted one.

In the context of religion, it may seem attractive to make religious faith seem less intellectual. Genuine faith in God should not need a theology degree. Although actions may speak louder than words, they should still ultimately be directed by principles. We need to understand the nature of the world in which we live and the role we play in it. Our actions should demonstrate what we truly believe, and rely on implicit or explicit attitudes to the world. Faith, of whatever kind, implies perseverance in the face of adversity, a belief in a truth that holds despite appearances. That may be admirable and virtuous, but there must be some grounding for such perseverance, some justification for it. Concentration on actions as a substitute for belief, rather than as an expression of it, ensures that one acts in a vacuum without clear reasons. Actions demonstrate faith, but faith should not be an arbitrary matter. Involving more than the intellect, it still needs rational grounding.

Degrees of faith

There is a cognitive element in faith, because faith needs a personal or collective understanding of what is or could be true. 'Belief' and 'faith' are often thought to be almost synonymous, and the words, as we shall continually see, almost seem interchangeable in ordinary speech. Yet this is to ignore important differences. A stress on 'belief' as a necessary component of faith can imply that one either believes something or does not, while faith itself can sometimes appear faltering. The opposite danger comes, when, so as not to make faith a purely intellectual matter, it is detached from any idea of perceived truth, and seems arbitrary or even positively irrational. The use of 'belief' as part of faith distinguishes the idea from that of complete knowledge. From the time of Plato, Greek philosophy saw that the distinction between knowledge and belief, even true belief, was very important, and this debate has continued into the modern age, as a keystone of epistemology. One problem is that 'belief' has become more and more constricted to refer in particular to a state

4

of mind rather than the whole stance of the person. Significantly the Greek word for faith in the original text of the New Testament, *pistis*, was not the word used by philosophers for a belief or opinion (*doxa*). As we have already seen, *pistis* in the ancient world often carried overtones of trust and loyalty. It is perhaps also relevant that the word 'creed', derived from the Latin *credo*, often itself carries overtones of trust and having confidence in someone or something, even putting one's heart into it. The word has etymological links with the Latin *cor* (heart).

Assimilating faith to belief makes it appear that having faith removes the possibility of doubt, so that one has a rational faith or no faith at all. The difficulty on that understanding is how to explain the cry of one man to Jesus in the New Testament when he said: 'I believe: help my unbelief.' The word used is the normal word for 'faith', so we could just as well understand the saying as 'I have faith: help my lack of faith'. While the former remark about belief might seem contradictory, it is striking that the cry of faith seems all too real to many people, who both have some faith and feel they need more. Faith can come in degrees much more readily than belief. I may not be certain it is raining but I cannot partially believe it is. I can have a faltering faith that allows room for doubt, and that is a common experience of even devout religious adherents.

Some forms of faith may seem more like the acceptance of the truth of certain claims, so that one acts accordingly, rather than necessarily having a firm belief that they are the case. Some philosophers adopt this position because they hold that belief is neither voluntary nor intentional, and they think that the idea of religious faith demands a deliberate personal commitment. An analogy might be a lawyer who accepts a client's version of events so as to present the case fairly in a court, while personally not having really to believe it. Even then, though, one might wonder if it is correct to say that the lawyer has any faith in the client's innocence. The lawyer would quite properly consider that the truth of the matter was for the court to decide, and not even have a view on the matter. How far mere acceptance sits easily with the idea of religious faith is more problematic. Without some personal investment in the idea of the truth of what is to be lived by, it would be hard to distinguish such a case from that of hypocrisy, of publicly acting in accord with beliefs one does not hold.

Faith involves reason, but involves more of our personality than this. Some contemporary philosophers wonder whether 'belief' properly describes even the rational element in faith. Faith can involve genuine belief and even apparent knowledge, but the word 'belief' can lead us to think that rational beliefs need proper evidence. It can sometimes appear in the Judaeo-Christian tradition that foundational religious beliefs must rest on evidence that can be rationally justified. It also sometimes seems as if faith exemplifies an attitude more like trust or hope. I may accept that something is true and hope that it is, but not be able to provide wholly convincing grounds for that belief. This all too easily enables many to dismiss religious faith as by definition irrational. While a cognitive element must be present in all faith, I can sometimes put my faith in something I cannot wholly justify rationally. Faith can never go against rationality, but paradoxically it can sometimes leap beyond the normal scope of human reason.

In cases of incomplete belief and knowledge, I often have to make a choice, particularly when it involves what I choose to be committed to through my life. Refusing to choose, as traditional agnosticism would have us do, is itself a choice not to live according to some possibilities. Faith may be compatible with a sense of uncertainty or with some feeling that God remains partly hidden. Indeed, faced with what by definition may transcend our knowledge, that feeling may be inevitable. Philosophers may be prone to assuming that faith must be an intellectual response to an assessment of available evidence. Other people's religious faith, however, may be influenced by wider factors such as the inspiring moral example of others, or the insight that religious teaching answers questions that otherwise cannot be answered. Faith, though, is more than mere hope, even if it can involve that. We can have idle hopes, but the idea of idle faith seems nonsensical. It requires definite action in a way that hope might not. On the other hand, 'blind' faith, without any accompanying notion that something could well be true, even if not wholly demonstrable, is no faith at all.

Some follow the 19th-century German philosopher Nietzsche and query the role not just of faith but of reason itself. They are often reacting to the 18th-century Enlightenment, which, in France at least, came close to deifying 'Reason', making churches and cathedrals 'Temples of Reason'. Even in the contemporary age there is great suspicion about the scope of reason, with many saying so-called disinterested reason is the tool of powerful economic or social interests. Reasoning can be made to be no more than the fact of different people, with different identities, reasoning in their own way, whose reason becomes more salient than its content. The idea of truth becomes inaccessible, and the only alternative, as indeed Nietzsche described, was the use of power by one group against another.

This attack on reason is particularly dangerous in the case of religion. It can be mercilessly attacked by those who may want to resist its alleged influence. Different religions and 'faith groups' can be pitted against each other, and conflict between, and within, religions can appear to be mere struggles for power. There must at least be the possibility of appealing to a rationality all can share, and an appreciation that some problems are universally shared. People of faith may feel that they can trust reason. Many philosophers, such as the 17th-century Oxford philosopher John Locke, have held that humans can trust reason because of its source in the divine Creator. Such rationality gives the possibility, at least in principle, for mutual dialogue and discussion. The very notion of rationality depends on understanding the difference between what is the case and what is not. A contemporary French philosopher of religion, Jean-Luc Marion, claims that 'in this time of nihilism one must maintain faith in reason itself'. He goes on to quote the French Jewish philosopher, Emmanuel Levinas, that the 'relations between religion and reason is not a problem of the philosophy of religion—it is philosophy itself'. All faith depends on reason but the alternative is not ungrounded faith but the inability to have faith in anything. The alternative to the possibility of truth must be nihilism, the idea that nothing is more true than anything else. Nothing matters.

The pursuit of truth

Truth cannot be jettisoned. Much, even within the apparent scope of science, can seem beyond our reach, as human beings. Knowledge can increase, but intrinsic human limitations can hold us back. All science needs the goal of truth, even when we cannot always grasp it, since that underpins the very idea of scientific progress. We cannot, as many do, pretend that truth is what people agree about. Mere consensus, and convention, whether in science or everyday life, do not guarantee that we have got things right. Even in science, present belief is often later recognized as deficient.

Reality can only be as we think it is if people construct their own worlds. When someone says, 'that is just your opinion', the implication is often that no opinion is better than another. Personal beliefs are then true for their holders, with no force for anyone else. I may not like bananas, but that does not mean that others will not enjoy them. Like tastes, my religious faith can be seen as a fact about me with no relevance for others, but this rejection of truth becomes self-defeating. Facts about people's faith themselves involve assertions about what people do or do not believe. They claim truth about people's attitudes. If I am wrong about what you believe, a gap opens between my belief and the true state of affairs. Similarly, even if moral beliefs do not claim

8

truth, there remains a question of the genuine nature of someone's moral attitudes. The idea of truth can never be totally discarded.

Denying truth means we can ignore awkward questions about the clash of faiths, and the need to resolve disagreements. Many are tempted by relativism, considering that the beliefs of a faith community may be true for it, if not for non-adherents. Beliefs of that kind are made into the conventions of a particular society, like rules of the road that in one nation demand people drive on the right, while in another all must go on the left. No truth is at stake, only an agreement that all should accept the same rules. The issue is whether faith is like that, something held to reinforce the solidarity of a group.

Even if it is agreed that there is a cognitive element in faith, which could fall short of full belief, we might still wonder about how far real doubt begins to undermine faith. Faith in any context involves risk because it is not the same as full knowledge. Can someone have faith in something but simultaneously doubt it? This is not a terminological question but one that many religious believers sometimes wrestle with. Many have worried that holding honest doubts involves disloyalty to their faith, and even to God. That means that they become afraid of admitting to real questions about the foundations of their faith. Some believers even see human reason as the enemy of faith. This can be a crucial question, because, for some religious doctrines, genuine faith can be linked to ideas of salvation. Lack of faith could, it appears, in the sight of God determine my future destiny. A strong faith may give courage to persevere in the face of difficulties, even of an intellectual kind, while critics can say that faith becomes irrational when a belief is held in the face of apparent evidence against it.

Religious beliefs are typically about what transcends human knowledge. Since, though, even when we have incomplete knowledge, paralysis is not an option, faith is often considered a virtue, particularly when what we are confronted with is, by definition, beyond our reach. Despite doubts and anxieties, a person of genuine religious faith may continue to live by what is hoped to be true. That may not amount to full-bodied belief, but there is still a necessary relationship between people's attitudes and their understanding of what might be true independently of them.

The fact that faith is regarded as a virtue suggests that it is under our own control, even if, for Christian doctrine, God's action in approaching us through 'grace' means that we have no right to feel self-satisfied or deserving of merit for our stance. Even so, many philosophers have argued that belief is not a voluntary matter. I believe something or I do not. I do not choose to see a red bus, as it is either presented to me or it is not. How then could we be blamed for a lack of initial belief in anything? Perhaps we can be held responsible for not putting ourselves in a position to acquire it, as when people refuse educational opportunities presented to them. This is the edge of perennial arguments about free will and determinism. The fundamental issue is that beliefs and other cognitive attitudes are orientated towards what is true. Faith, and especially religious faith, implies a positive attitude to claims about truth in an area, ruling out subjectivist views of faith which see it as being simply a property of persons and a description of their attitudes.

Nihilism and power

Religious practices and rituals can give identity to a group but not be of any concern to those outside it. Some religions could see rituals as an end in themselves. Participation, not belief, would be what counts. In the Roman Empire, members of the infant Christian Church invited trouble by refusing to sacrifice to the Emperor. Yet the beliefs that could underlie the ritual and the implications of calling the Emperor 'divine' did not unduly worry Romans. The act of sacrifice indicated loyalty, as standing respectfully for a national anthem today might. It signified an acknowledgement of the political authority of Rome. Christians, with clear beliefs about one Creator, requiring exclusive worship, did not see the ritual like that. Its significance could not be divorced from the issue of truth.

Any religious practice can be regarded as a mere public ceremony, but only makes sense in the context of wider belief. One can enjoy a particular form of worship because of the intrinsic beauty of its music, without subscribing to the beliefs behind it. Sincere participation in it, however, entails complex beliefs, which should be expressed in behaviour beyond worship. Beliefs about what is true underlie religious ceremonies and rituals. The expression of faith involves a proclamation of identity, showing what I agree with and the people with whom I am aligned. Even so, the stance of faith implies that we all ultimately face a world that none of us has constructed. We must live our life one way or another, and that involves choices about the kind of world we think we inhabit.

Nihilism involves a reaction against this way of thinking. Its denial that there is any common reality, universal truth, or even a single human nature still leaves us with a decision on how to live. If literally nothing matters, and no purpose is better than any other, why choose anything? It is like driving into a vast empty car park without a reason for choosing one space rather than another. Indecision can result in paralysis. This problem goes deep and brings us to the possibility of language and communication itself. How can we teach a language unless we are all deemed to confront the same phenomena, and recognize them in the same way? How can I teach my child what a dog is if I cannot be sure there is such a thing as a dog? A nihilist, and even a sceptic, would say that because no one is able to stand outside all beliefs and decide which are right, there can be no such thing as being right. Consciousness of fallibility should not produce total despair. We all make mistakes, but that does not stop us recognizing what is true, and, sometimes in retrospect, what was an error. Faith in any context helps us to leap beyond the knowledge we presently have and can be a spur to further progress.

Reason can ground faith, while some just rely on authority, believing what they are told by others. The first possibility was stressed in the Enlightenment of the 17th and 18th centuries. At first, in 17th-century England, after the Civil War, belief in the power of human reason appeared an integral part of Christian faith, both following from it and giving it direction. Modern science could properly be said to begin with scientists, such as Isaac Newton, exploring and explaining regularities of the universe, by means of human reason and observation. They were motivated by faith in an ordered Creation, planned by a divine law-giver.

Thinkers craved for peaceful ways of settling disputes and acquiring knowledge. The devastation of war had demonstrated the dire consequences of relying on force to solve disagreements. John Locke stressed the importance of toleration, particularly in religious matters. His writings were much later to be a formative influence on the founding of the United States, and were a huge influence on Thomas Jefferson, the primary author of the American Declaration of Independence. Locke grew up in a Somerset village south of the important city of Bristol, and would have seen the sky glowing red from fires set off in the city during the Civil War. Three hundred years later the same thing happened, reflecting fires devastating Bristol's heart in the bombing of the Second World War. Might was still trying to prove it was right.

Religious disagreements played their part in the English Civil War, with opponents and supporters of the established Church of England making their differing views all too apparent. Puritanism, rooted in religion, and Parliamentarianism, rooted in views of government, were intermingled. Views of the source of national authority, and of authority within the Church, were at times hard to separate, and fanaticism could flourish and spawn violence. Any question can become a matter of who has most power, and Locke and his contemporaries saw reason as the alternative. The Royal Society was established in London in 1660 after the Restoration of the monarchy. It was not founded because of blind faith in science and its methods but relied on a prior trust in the role of human reason as a way of dispassionately deciding what was the case. That acted as a check on claims to certainty of the kind that had led to violence and destruction. It was a way of testing claims to arbitrary authority, but was not an alternative to religious faith, as it explicitly depended on the idea of reason as a gift of God.

The later Enlightenment in 18th-century France was explicit in its distrust of claims to religious authority, particularly as embodied in the Roman Catholic Church. Rationalism became associated with a sceptical, even atheist, attitude. The centrality of human beings and human reason was stressed, in a way that left little room for belief in a transcendent reality. In the latter part of the 20th century, many became distrustful of this 'modern' conception of some universal reason. Some saw it as arbitrarily giving 'Reason' itself the authority previously attributed to God. They echo the German philosopher, Friedrich Nietzsche, who, in the 19th century, mentioned in his *Notebooks* that 'there are no facts, only interpretations'. He perversely added 'and this is an interpretation'. All claims are bound, it seems, by the assumptions of a tradition or perspective, and can never break free to claim what is universally valid. Appeals to truth then only become assertions of power by individuals or groups.

This distrust of appeals to a timeless rationality, and of the possibility of being open to a reality beyond ourselves, became the hallmark of what has become known as post-modernism. It reacted against the Enlightenment ideal of a universally applicable rationality, by insisting that reasoning, even in modern science, is conditioned by time and place. Nietzsche was consistent in his belief that all is interpretation. We never get through the veil of our own understanding, with the object of faith always defined and established by that faith. That claim itself becomes an assertion of some faith and we are caught in a dizzying regress whereby nothing can be finally accepted as the case. Everything is dependent on a background, which itself depends on a further background. We stand on the edge of an abyss so that no belief can be stated, and no faith expressed, without being referred beyond itself. Nothing can be accepted in the terms on which it is put forward. The inevitable result is that language must finally give way to silence, with nothing communicated, and any action as good or bad as any other. We need a grounding, some place on which we can stand. 'Modernism' certainly provided one such place with its faith in a rationality that could be universally valid and expressed through the methods of contemporary science.

Post-modernism asked where the proponents of Enlightenment rationality themselves stood. What justified their faith in the universality of reason and its ability to extract itself from the prejudices of time and place? Human rationality took the place of a God that could see everything, with what philosophers have sometimes called a 'God's eye view'. Human reason could then replace God as our guide. If, though, as Nietzsche maintained, the pursuit of reason is shackled by human limitations, and even formed by processes outside its own consciousness, reliance on its influence is illusory. All that is left is the power that humans may themselves possess over each other. Nietzsche extolled what he called a 'will to power', a philosophy later eagerly seized on by German fascism. The argument against reason dissolved itself in self-contradiction. We are always referred back to speakers and their background. The subject is always changed from what a faith is about to whose faith it is.

The 'hermeneutics of suspicion'

Nietzsche has been coupled with Karl Marx and Sigmund Freud as a proponent of what the 20th-century French philosopher Paul

Ricoeur called the 'hermeneutics of suspicion'. The phrase has been readily adopted and applies particularly to the unmasking of beliefs. They could hide deeper motivations of which the subject may be unaware. Marx's theories suggest that people may be driven by the pursuit of class advantage. Nietzsche saw only the underlying desire for domination through power. For Freud, the unconscious motivations might be sexual, operating on an individual rather than social basis. None of these see beliefs as the result of some truth conveyed to us, or some object revealed. They are products of drives within us which may or may not be ultimately revealed. Our conscious thoughts cannot be taken at face value since they are caused by some other force. This encouraged scepticism and each theory saw religious belief as a particular target. The assumption was that there could be no divine revelation, but that humans must believe in God because of some psychological or social need.

This kind of analysis is widespread, even when people do not consciously follow the thought of one of these 19th-century thinkers. Social structures that may give an advantage to one group are regularly invoked to explain apparent prejudices. For example, the idea of 'structural racism' can suggest deep, but unconscious, motivations for some attitudes. A belief becomes a disguise for something else. Ricoeur himself says that this makes us sceptical of 'the given'. We cannot open ourselves to the truth because inbuilt biases encourage us to believe what we want. Interestingly he says: 'the contrary of suspicion, I will say bluntly, is faith'. He maintains that it is a 'rational faith' because its interpretation (or hermeneutics) is directed at an object. In his words, such hermeneutics wants 'to describe and not to reduce'. Faith is necessary because of the assumption that a symbol such as a word can be 'a cultural mechanism for apprehension of reality, as a place of revelation'. We have to assume there is something speaking to us, or something we can listen to, rather than everything being a mere reflection of our own desires and needs. Ricoeur has religious belief in mind, as is demonstrated by his careful use of the term 'revelation', as well as his appeal to faith. It is not only in religion that faith must be open to something beyond itself.

For Ricoeur, language is the all-important medium, and hermeneutics is the interpretation of language. He believes, though, that language is not free-floating, but refers to something. Language is not so much spoken by us as 'spoken to' us. We are, he says 'born into language, into the light of the logos "who enlightens every man who comes into the world"'. In this reference to St John's opening words in his Gospel, Ricoeur follows the linguistic bias of much modern philosophy, particularly in France. Following its origins in biblical interpretation, hermeneutics is concerned with understanding texts and language. Yet 'logos', though often translated as 'word', has a considerable hinterland in Greek philosophy, even before Plato. It carried with it the whole idea of reasoning, so that the term 'logic' is derived from it. St John was himself aware of these resonances and equated 'logos' with the underlying 'reason' or rational scheme behind all things, indeed even with God. The notion of an objective order, open to our understanding, is very prominent.

God and reason

The hermeneutics of suspicion turned its back not only on faith in God, but on faith in reason itself. Earlier thinkers coupled their trust in the power of human rationality with faith in God. They thought that humans, made in the image of God, could think God's thoughts after Him, particularly in studying the works of Creation through science. They could read the 'Book of Nature' written by the Creator, just as they read that other Book, the Bible, recounting God's special revelation. This was encapsulated by the slogan of the so-called 'Cambridge Platonists', a group of philosophers and theologians based in Cambridge in the middle of the 17th century, influential in the founding of the Royal Society.

For them, reason was 'the candle of the Lord'. That was the maxim of Benjamin Whichcote, whose church John Locke later attended in London. It appears in a stained-glass window commemorating Whichcote in the Chapel of Emmanuel College, Cambridge. The phrase anchors trust in reason to God, but warns us that reason is not a glaring searchlight removing all doubt. It is a pale, flickering light casting many shadows.

Locke himself echoed this, when he refers to the 'parties of men', who 'cram their tenets down all men's throats whom they can get in their power'. They do not, he claims, allow truth to have 'fair play', nor humans the 'liberty to search after it'. He proclaims that most would be in darkness, under bondage, 'were not the candle of the Lord set up by himself in men's minds, which it is impossible for the breath or power of man wholly to extinguish'. A God-given reason is, he thought, a bulwark against the arbitrary use of power. It was a guarantee for the scientists founding the Royal Society that not only was the world rationally ordered, but they had the means to begin to understand its workings. As the image of the candle suggests, steps towards knowledge will be tentative and provisional. We find out how the world works by observation and by experimenting with its constituents. The complexity of the contingent, changing, environment we inhabit as humans cannot give us the certainty of mathematics.

The image of the candle, giving partial but incomplete illumination, suggests that the operation of reason eventually involves taking something on trust. Faith and reason are inter-dependent, and cannot easily be separated. Faith involves a rational specification about what we believe in. Faith in God is empty unless we have some idea of what we mean by God, and some understanding of the way of life that faith might involve. Religious faith must make a difference to people's lives, but the way it is directed, and why, involves the operation of human reason.

If reason is independent of specific revelation, and can underpin religious faith, discussion of religion is not confined to participants in that religion, let alone theologians. Faith needs reason, and reason appears an integral constituent of human nature, so general philosophical reflection on matters concerning religion can be appropriate. The Protestant theologian of the mid-20th century, Karl Barth, gave priority to the idea of revelation, particularly through Christ and the proclamation of the Christian Gospel. He did not want a philosophical foundation for religious belief. The idea of natural knowledge, expressed by the discipline of natural theology, and the philosophy of religion more generally, suggests the possibility of such reasoning. Human reason has an independent validity, and, even without any direct knowledge of God, it is claimed that it can understand the possible place of a Creator in the scheme of things. That is essential if the universal claims of any religion are not to be ignored. Religions typically point towards a transcendent reality, separate from the physical world and hence 'metaphysical'. That idea of transcendence inevitably entails the idea of universality. What is beyond full human comprehension, and is independent of humans, must have a relevance for all, and not just for those who 'construct' beliefs about it. What is true, wherever truth lies, remains so even for those who do not recognize that truth.

From the standpoint of Roman Catholicism, Pope John Paul II said in his encyclical letter *Faith and Reason* (*Fides et Ratio*) that in the light of the knowledge conferred by faith, there emerge certain truths which 'reason from its own independent enquiry already perceives'. Because of this, the Pope stressed the fundamental importance of philosophy for theological studies. There is a place, he thought, for reason in the examination of the credentials of faith. That view is supported by the belief that a rationality held by all humans is not the enemy of faith, but is the gift of a God who created all 'in His image'.

Religion's fear of reason

Some religious believers, not just in Christianity, are afraid of the power of reason, and fear it has religion at its mercy, rather than being its support. It is important for any faith that minds can be prepared to recognize the possibility of divine revelation. Even so the role of philosophy has remained controversial. Pope John Paul II was following the mediaeval theologian St Thomas Aquinas on the role of philosophy because they both trusted human rationality as itself a gift of God. Others, such as John Calvin, a giant of the 16th-century Protestant Reformation in Europe, have been more distrustful. For Calvin, philosophy was the expression of human vanity, and attempted independence from God and divine revelation. Reason was contaminated by human sin, and philosophy, as the specialized product of such reason, was going to be especially dangerous, and corrupted by human degeneration.

Calvin thought that human hearts are already inscribed with some glimmering of knowledge about God, a sense of deity (*sensus divinitatis*). He found it difficult to see that human rationality could have similar divine origins, although his own reasoning about the respective roles of reason and faith was itself an example of the power of human reason. If all human reason has to be distrusted, so must all theological reasoning. For Calvin, we only understand by faith, so that we have 'no eyes to perceive' until enlightened by internal revelation by God, particularly through Scripture. That leaves unanswered the question why the exercise of human reason cannot also itself be the result of a more general divine revelation, as the idea of reason as 'the candle of the Lord' suggests.

Discussions about the role of reason and human philosophy go to the heart of basic ideas of human nature and its relation to religious faith. Is that to be seen as the product of a free and responsible choice for which we are accountable to God, or as an apparently arbitrary gift from God to the chosen few, seen by Calvinists as 'the Elect'? Does Christianity preach a Gospel for all, or is it confined to the lucky few who are chosen? Reason has universal applicability, but faith, when bestowed on particular people, could be seen as the privileged possession of those chosen through 'divine grace'. This argument concerns the universal applicability of the Christian gospel, and the significance for everyone of the transcendence of God.

This has led to complicated theological arguments over the centuries within Christianity, but the role of reason as a basis for theology, preceding revelation, surfaces in other religions and has at times done so in Islam. Greek philosophy influenced Islamic theology in its early days in the 8th century, and also later in the person of Ibn Rashid (Averroes). In 12th-century Muslim Spain, he was a famous commentator on Aristotle. The place of philosophy, and indeed of a rational theology, has been challenged throughout the history of Islam, so that the predominant stress has been on obedience to divine revelation through the Qur'an, and subsequent texts, Hadiths, which relate oral traditions about the words and deeds of the Prophet Muhammad. The picture that emerged was that of God issuing commands that demanded unquestioning obedience. Such texts tended to show Muslims what to believe, but not why they should believe it. To question God's revealed will was to be disobedient, and an independent human rationality could not provide an alternative source of knowledge, as the result of a free search for understanding. It was not in a position to validate basic belief.

The corollary was that faith was not a matter of individual choice, but a corporate possession, with a focus on legal requirements for proper behaviour. Thus, a contemporary Muslim writer, Mustafa Akyol, is able to claim that a 'soldier-like obedience to religious texts reflects the mainstream religious mindset in broad parts of the Muslim world today'. For many Muslims, external law, and the jurisprudence associated with it, has a validity prior to the individual conscience. Obedience to divine commands, understood through the received interpretation of texts, is recognized as the dominant virtue. Little room is left for individual moral choice, or any independent rational assessment of what is true. For many orthodox Muslims through the centuries, philosophy has seemed to threaten the faith of believers. Against such a background, the loss of personal faith, through apostasy, or its repudiation through blasphemy, are treated with severity in many Islamic regimes. They seem to challenge the very basis of society, having a legal structure stemming from *sharia* law. A personally adopted faith can be regarded as an impious challenge to the will of God.

Without any appeal to universal standards of reason, this stress on obedience can appear to be a resort to power and compulsion by those in authority. This is in spite of a much-quoted saying in the Qu'ran that 'there is no compulsion in religion'. Appeals to the importance of individual freedom and rationality, and to the value of personal faith, can be dismissed in Islamic societies as the result of the suspicious entry of alien, probably Western, ideals. The role of reason in religion, and its connection with faith, is an issue that cannot go away. It lies at the root of the self-understanding of both Christianity and Islam, and must always be a factor in any religious belief.

Chapter 2
Faith and God

Knowledge and experience

Everything cannot be perpetually questioned. In any sphere, we need firm ground and start with a faith in something. If we are scientists, we take the existence of the world we investigate for granted. We assume its regularity, and our ability to generalize, saying that because certain empirical regularities hold here or now, they will also hold there or then. Physicists refer to the far reaches of the universe, even when they lie beyond all possible observation, and assume the same physical laws hold everywhere in it. Contemporary science shows its willingness to depend on theories that can only indirectly be confirmed by scientific procedures. When physicists produce speculative theories about the existence of alternative universes, they deal with what transcends actual human knowledge, but also goes beyond any possible knowledge, gained through observation or experiment. Alternative universes may even depend on different physical laws, in no way comparable to those with which we are familiar.

Sometimes physicists postulate universes as existing merely because they are judged possible because of mathematical calculations, and then the constraints of human observation are left far behind. Physics also reaches for the infinitesimally small, as the basis for the construction of matter, beyond the hope of any direct scientific verification. Contemporary scientists often conceive of realities that are almost beyond human understanding. The idea of an infinite number of universes certainly transcends the limits of our knowledge. Yet that used to be the objection made against all so-called 'metaphysics' by scientifically minded philosophers. Logical positivists, who were influential in philosophy after the Second World War, were inspired by the meetings of the Vienna Circle, a group of philosophers of science meeting in Vienna before the war. For them science determined not just truth, but also what could be meaningful in language. If we do not know how to check something scientifically, we cannot, they maintained, talk about it. Their stress on scientific verifiability, though, cannot even be applied properly to contemporary physics, with its reliance on purely theoretical entities. Indeed, the criterion of verifiability cannot itself be verified. It may simply be regarded as an axiom, but then there seems little reason to adopt it as it arbitrarily cuts out so much of human experience in ethics and aesthetics as well as religion.

Hard-nosed empiricism lives on in scepticism about how humans can have any comprehension of a non-material reality. Even so, if physics can talk of other universes that appear to transcend human understanding, even a divine reality cannot be excluded by definition. If all knowledge must be derived directly from the bedrock of human sense experience, any reality which goes beyond or transcends it becomes intrinsically unknowable and irrelevant to human life. That applies equally to the objects of physics and to the God of monotheism. For many, though, faith in science and its capabilities reigns supreme, so that 'non-physical', or 'spiritual', entities are defined out of existence.

The impact of empiricist philosophy, linking science simply to what humans experience through their senses, lives on under the banner of 'naturalism'. It has had its influence within Christian theology. The verificationists of the Vienna Circle frightened many religious believers, even theologians, with their insistence that what could not be specified in scientific terms was meaningless. Faith in God seemed tantamount to faith in nothing. A reaction to this onslaught on the possibility of a separate realm, existing apart from our material world, was a radical theology that tried to reinterpret Christianity in terms that did not involve such claims. This was epitomized in popular consciousness in the 1960s in Britain by a book, *Honest to God*, by the Anglican Bishop of Woolwich, John Robinson. After deriding a view of a God 'up there in the heavens', he attacked the idea of a God who is spiritually or metaphysically 'out there'. He seemed at times to be questioning the relevance to Christian belief of the idea of a God as Creator who was separate from the material world. Robinson's favourite way of describing God, following the theologian Paul Tillich, was of God as 'the ground of our Being', a phrase that appeared to link God too much with human existence.

Echoes of this surface in contemporary theology and philosophy of religion. Can we hold to any religious belief while adopting a scientific view of human beings as natural beings in the natural world? Fiona Ellis, a philosopher of religion, suggests that 'we avoid metaphysical flights of fancy and ensure that our own claims remain empirically grounded'. She seems to accept the worldview of science but still finds room for God within it. That is a difficult task. She wants to say that 'God and the world do not add up to two', because we do not know God 'as an object among others'. This claim that God is not an object is often produced in modern thought. Since the nature of God must be radically different from that of ordinary physical objects, it seems uncontroversial. It can slide into the idea that God is not really 'objective', and not there independent of us. The issue turns to the nature of our faith as it is lived out in our lives, rather than the possible focus of our faith.

God is not one entity amongst others, nor part of the furniture of the universe, or multi-verse. Phrases, though, such as 'the ground of our being', or even references to 'Being' itself, are so vague that it becomes unclear what a religious believer has faith in. The verificationist accusation of the meaninglessness of religious language can seem apposite. If someone claims there is a 'heffalump' in the garden, it is crucial to be able to recognize it. What does it look like? What does it smell like? What noise does it make? What tracks does it leave? Unless these questions can be answered, it becomes impossible to identify one at all. Something that is invisible, intangible, odourless, and leaves no traces might not seem very different from nothing at all. The challenge has always been whether God is like that.

The pragmatist outlook

The Vienna Circle reacted to the growth in human knowledge brought by science, by adopting a 'scientific world conception' that left no room for metaphysics in general, and God in particular. At the same time in the United States, scepticism about metaphysical speculation was encouraged by American pragmatist philosophy. It was epitomized by the work of William James in the late 19th century and the beginning of the 20th, and was taken up later by others including John Dewey. In a series of lectures at Yale University, significantly entitled *A Common Faith*, Dewey interpreted all faith in terms of its 'function' in life. For him the crucial issue was not what faith purported to be about, but the role that faith plays in the lives of people of faith. In this he was allied to the verificationist approach, deriding claims about realities beyond human reach. The pragmatist concern was the difference beliefs made to people's lives. That was their 'cash-value', and their importance.

The function of faith, or its role in people's lives, then becomes its justification. Entertaining certain ideas in such circumstances becomes a means to other, perhaps desirable, ends. Faith floats free of its cognitive element, and it can be difficult to distinguish the situation from that of someone who merely pretends to believe, or the hypocrite who deliberately wishes to deceive others.

Genuine faith might involve an element of hope but it is incompatible with actual disbelief in its claims. Someone who pragmatically goes along with them because of the effects they produce in lives might be doing something that is in the end ineffective. Religious commitment can be costly and without the beliefs that inspires it, it might not seem worth persevering with.

Dewey himself denied that religious qualities and values were bound up 'with any single item of intellectual assent'. What mattered was not what beliefs were about (including God) but the actions in which they were expressed. For Dewey, faith meant the identification of the self with various ideal ends. A stress on faith including the whole person was significant, but so was the demotion of religious doctrines to the status of ideals. Doctrines claim truth, but ideals are defined by their influence on a person's behaviour. Pragmatism is a down-to-earth philosophy, but its problem in interpreting religion is that no religion, whatever its relevance for life, is merely 'down-to-earth'.

Religion points to the transcendent, and if that is a fruitless exercise, as the verificationists maintained, it will not be helped by pretending that any religion is just about following ideals in life. Dewey rejected the idea of any special truth promulgated by religion, but held to what he calls 'the reality of ideal ends and values', pointing to the authority they appear to exert over us. He repudiated dogma and doctrine, but still assumed that basic values have a hold over our humanity. He talked of justice and affection, and the correspondence of ideas 'with realities that we call truth'. That sounds very fine, but Dewey was lecturing in a society with seemingly settled views on such matters. He was able to put a pragmatist spin on the liberal Protestant theology that stressed moral and social action rather than doctrine, while still showing the influence of that doctrine. Assuming agreement on basic moral principles, Dewey thought that the ethical core of religion, particularly Christianity, could survive, while conceding the intellectual ground to what he termed the 'naturalistic' assumptions of modern science. Even if dogma about the supernatural could be forgotten, he imagined the life of faith could continue, because he changed the meaning of 'faith'.

Pragmatist intuitions continue to have influence. There is a tendency to see the importance of faith as a guide to action, not a claim to special truth. Through the influences of pragmatism and empiricism, there is an urge to reinterpret, or even forget, claims to supernatural intervention or miracles. It seems easier to concentrate on the beneficial effects of faith, any faith, on lives. Like Thomas Jefferson, who rewrote the Gospels to exclude miraculous events, many have assumed that the ethical content of Christianity, and other religions, could stand on its own, without doctrinal, or metaphysical, support. As religious influence has waned in many countries, that cannot be taken for granted. Increasing diversity and moral disagreement indicates otherwise.

The attraction of 'fideism'

Reference to a transcendent being (or 'Being') may seem to have no content. Even if faith in God can make a difference to people's lives, and is 'real' for them, we still face the question whether that engages with anything real beyond ourselves. Perhaps we ought to concentrate on the mere fact of our belief and not what it is about. A recurring philosophical approach to faith takes its mere existence as crucial, and refuses to link it with the demands of rational justification. Dubbed 'fideism' (from the Latin for 'faith', *fides*), it is a recurring view in the history of the philosophy of religion, and appeared most recently through the influence of the later work, over the last two generations, of the Austrian philosopher (turned Cambridge Professor), Ludwig Wittgenstein.

The use of the word 'faith' can be contrasted not just with reason, but with the possibility of proof. The urge to prove God's existence is bolstered by the notion that God's existence is not contingent, but necessary. He seemingly must exist and be self-sufficient and ontologically separate from the contingent world. One proof of God's existence was the traditional ontological argument of St Anselm of Canterbury, in the 11th century. He famously claimed to derive the existence of God from the concept of 'a being than which no greater can be conceived'. His arguments provided centuries of debate, and held that a perfect Being that did not exist was less great than one who did. The idea was that existence could be derived from the concept of perfection. That kind of argument seems to leave little room for faith. We either see its truth or just cannot, like a child who finds simple arithmetic difficult to grasp. Many philosophers, however, have pointed out that existence is not a quality or characteristic that can be added to an entity. A tree at the corner of the street that happens not to exist would be no tree at all.

If God exists, that does not mean that we, from our standpoint, can *prove* He exists. There may be indications of His existence such as the apparent order and regularity of the world that forms the basis of science. Some would argue that there is an ultimate First Cause, but the fact that we stop somewhere in causal explanations does not mean that we must stop in the same single place. A materialist or naturalistic desire to see the physical world as the ultimate fact is not a logical contradiction. Where we decide to stop itself becomes a matter of faith. We need eventually to put our trust in something or somebody, even if it is in the operation of reason itself.

Wittgenstein's later philosophy reacted against the science-based philosophy of the logical positivists in the Vienna Circle, even though his earlier views had appeared to support it. His lectures about religion highlighted an important fact about religious belief. He saw that, while empirical evidence, even from history, might allegedly provide reasons for belief, something was missing. Assent to alleged facts does not take us very far. For him, language gains its meaning from how it is used in different contexts that give meaning, and how it is embedded in people's lives.

Faith in God may then become a decision to live a particular kind of life, involving no metaphysical speculation. Wittgenstein says that people who see things in a religious way think differently, say different things to themselves, and have different pictures in their minds. Someone might imagine the Last Judgement and believe that all are called to account for their lives before God. For Wittgenstein, our faith consists of adopting a way of life in the light of the pictures which we entertain. The pictures are part of our pattern of life, an indispensable element in the 'form of life' we are committed to.

This approach to religion led to a significant dispute amongst philosophers of religion in the closing decades of the 20th century. Some saw religious faith as part of a way of life, but others saw religious beliefs as essentially making claims about truth. The issue was once again whether religious faith is significant because of what it claims to be about, or whether its nature is grounded in the way people behave.

Risk and freedom

Philosophers of religion often warn of the dangers of thinking that religious belief is just an explanatory scientific hypothesis, trying to explain the origins of the cosmos and of human life. One contemporary philosopher, John Cottingham, warns that 'knowledge of God is all too often assimilated to the kind of knowledge science seeks to achieve'. Surely, he suggests, faith is concerned with moral transformation. 'Existentialist' philosophers have tried to concentrate on our own existence and its meaning for us, rather than with vague gestures to something beyond. A major influence in the field of religion was the Danish philosopher, Kierkegaard, who in the 19th century was scornful of what he termed 'speculative philosophy'. In remarks that have a resonance in the 21st century, he alleged that, because of our vastly increased knowledge, particularly in science, 'men had forgotten what it means to *exist* and what *inwardness* signifies'.

He talks of the uncertainty of the truth of Christianity, and instead stressed the role of the subject, and the 'inwardness' of the faith of the believer. It was a matter of the heart, not speculation. When Kierkegaard says that 'without risk there is no faith', he seems to indicate that faith can be about something that we can be wrong about. Yet he still stressed the inwardness and subjectivity of faith.

Kierkegaard's concern with the inward depths of human existence can make truth the creation of individuals for themselves. It encourages a subjectivism that foreshadows later forms of existentialist philosophy in the 20th century. If, though, we follow Wittgenstein and his stress on social context and 'forms of life', we arrive at a relativism in which meaning is constructed within a collective way of life and is incomprehensible to those outside. Both views fail to take seriously the transcendent reality of God, which outstrips our beliefs about Him. That apparent inaccessibility has meant that many turn away from an object of religious faith which seems to recede beyond the horizon. The 'otherness' of such divine reality is stressed by the incongruity of even referring to God as 'He'. While many see this as objectionable, and 'patriarchal', God, particularly in the Christian tradition, has been seen as personal, and personified as a loving, heavenly Father. The English language cannot refer to a person without a gender, and this itself illustrates the inadequacy of language when confronted with the alleged reality of the divine.

The gap between human understanding and the reality of God must be bridged, and finite human minds cannot accomplish that on their own. Any theological account of God has to explain both why there is a gap and how it could be crossed. If there is a loving God, why would He not want us to have some knowledge of Him, and make it easier for us to have faith in Him? Some wonder why faith should be necessary at all, involving the risk of a leap into the uncertainty referred to by Kierkegaard.

The presence of human freedom, or free will, can be a philosophical answer to the apparent absence of firm knowledge of God. We are not, it is claimed, automata, or puppets on strings manipulated by a divine master of ceremonies. We are not caused to be certain kinds of people or have particular beliefs. The freedom lying at the heart of that understanding of human nature guarantees the possibility of rationality. Caused beliefs can be accidentally true, but their causes may be unrelated to any question of truth. Why we believe and what we believe need have little connection with each other, as the hermeneutics of suspicion illustrated. All reasoning could be like the results of post-hypnotic suggestion. For example, a person can be told under hypnosis that on coming out of a trance, he or she will look for an umbrella and open it out in the room they are in. That is what duly happens, but when asked why they are doing it, they will always give a spurious explanation, perhaps saying that they need to check it was not damaged. That is a rationalization produced by a causal influence outside their knowledge. Any deterministic theory concentrating on causes, rather than reasons for belief, suggests that all reasoning is mere rationalization like this.

Freedom and rationality go together, but freedom comes at a cost. Once we have the power to reason, freely choosing between alternatives, everyone can go wrong. We may have inadequate information, or wilfully follow our own interests rather than inconvenient truths. That can even happen when scientists confront the physical world. Once humans are faced with what lies beyond that, whether possible universes or a transcendent God who created us, it looks as if we are all groping into the dark. It is a basic tenet for Christians and Jews that God made us in His own image, granting humans the ability to recognize truth, and reason towards it. With that rationality goes the freedom to abuse it. The question is how, as finite creatures, we can make the leap from the familiar world of sights and sounds to anything lying beyond. In science, this requires years of training. Scientific belief does not come naturally, and scientists learn to accept counter-intuitive ideas that lie beyond common sense. Science still claims to bring us into contact with realities. Is religious faith similar, or is it 'just' a matter of training and upbringing? An unkind word for that is indoctrination.

Because religious faith involves a risky leap into what seems unknown, it can be dismissed as irrational. The constant refrain is that faith involves commitments to what cannot be established by reason. This bleak contrast between faith and reason haunts all discussion of religious faith. Even if faith has its reasons, are they the result of rationalization? Others can say that because the transcendent is intrinsically mysterious, the only recourse is to some form of 'negative theology', saying what God is not. That just maintains that God is so utterly different from us that we can say nothing positive about 'Him', 'Her', 'It', or whatever. The consequence is that such vacuity leaves us with nothing in which to have faith.

Chapter 3
Faith and diversity

Is religious belief natural?

Religious belief, in many forms, has been a universal feature of human life. After the collapse of Communism in countries which had been made officially atheist, there was often a resurgence of overt belief. Anthropologists can always be certain that whatever human society they study, some religion would have played a part. Archaeologists may not always uncover religious buildings, but they can see signs of religion, such as in burial customs.

Why should religion be so universal? We seem to be born with religious beliefs of an unformed nature. They are innate, and we appear to have a natural intimation of divinity. Despite his empiricist philosophy, John Locke believed in the power of a reason emanating from God. He proclaimed that 'reason is natural revelation', and defined revelation as 'natural reason enlarged by a new set of discoveries communicated by God immediately, which reason vouches the truth of'. While rationality was in the category of general revelation from God to everyone, there was also 'special revelation'. This came to particular people such as prophets, through Christ, or by means of insights given to ordinary individuals. Knowledge of God, whether through direct experience or indirect reasoning, can never, it is alleged, be produced by human abilities alone, but through divine initiative.

If we are made in the image of God, and share, however imperfectly, divine freedom and rationality, we should be able to reach out towards God, and even have some innate tendency to be able to conceive of a divinity. That is rejected by an empiricist, for whom all knowledge comes from experience. Modern research in cognitive science relies on neo-Darwinian ideas of genetic influence. It alleges that the human mind is not a 'blank slate' but may already be predisposed, perhaps for evolutionary reasons, towards some form of religious belief. The cognitive architecture of the human mind may be biased so that it becomes easy to think of God or the supernatural. For example, people find it natural to think of humans surviving death. Hence ancestors are worshipped. Humans have always quickly interpreted events in terms of personal agency and have easily seen the rustling of trees or the motion of the sea as purposefully motivated. That no doubt explains the origin of beliefs in tree-spirits, or ancient gods of the sea such as Poseidon or Neptune.

Cross-cultural evidence even seems to suggest that children find it natural to think in ways that lead to religious ways of thought. They may not be born with fully fledged ideas of God but are still inclined to see physical processes in terms of purpose. They may say that rocks are pointed so that birds may not sit on them. Children, too, can think of God as 'all-knowing' in the way that they, at least at first, thought their parents were. A simple experiment demonstrates this. If an apple is placed under one of two cups in front of a mother but moved under the other one when she has left the room, a child of 3 will claim that Mummy will know where the apple is now, when she returns. At the age of 4, when children have developed what has been called a 'theory of mind', they will realize that Mummy does not know everything, and will be mistaken about where the apple now is. Yet they may still find it natural to envisage a God who does know everything. The point is not what children are taught, let alone what is true. It is simply what they can go on finding it easy to understand.

Empirical research in cognitive psychology and anthropology uncovers cultural traits, like these, that appear to be universal, and lead to basic impulses that can produce religious belief. The human mind seems primed to look for the existence of the divine. The very empirical science that can at times reject ideas of the supernatural also points to the existence of innate tendencies that encourage us to think of it. Such dispositions are more significant in moulding human society than has often been accepted. None of this proves, or disproves, the existence of the divine. It merely suggests that human nature is naturally ready to accept religious explanations. Which ones are adopted will depend on other factors, not just social, but also the availability of different forms of apparent revelation. For good or ill, we all appear to be born with a 'god-shaped' hole in our minds waiting to be filled. Humans are naturally inclined to be religious.

Religious faith, of any kind, is in this way deeply rooted in the way humans are. Some may accept that we have such tendencies, but hold they are 'infantile', and we should grow out of them. Others could say that if we believe in a God as Creator, we might expect that He would give us the capability, which presumably animals do not have, of grasping the idea of a God, or at least of divinity. Freedom and responsibility for our choices would mean little if we could not grasp the meaning of choices before us. We might, too, expect that, if there is a God, and He wishes us to approach Him, humans would be prepared for divine revelation, both from the nature of the world, and more directly. God may have left us free, it may be said, but He did not leave us in complete darkness.

Faith and different religions

We may see common strands in our behaviour as humans, and these may enable us to understand those who seem superficially very different from us. We can see similarities between diverse forms of religious faith but must be wary of interpreting everything in terms that we are familiar with in our own society.

Not everything will make sense when seen exclusively through the concepts of the modern Western world. This raises questions about the very possibility of disciplines such as social anthropology and comparative religion. We can, for instance, too easily assume that concepts familiar in a Christian, or post-Christian, background apply to very different societies and religions. The word 'faith' provides a salient example. It is so central for many centuries of Christian theology that using it in other religious contexts can lead us to unconsciously assume some form of Christian understanding. Forcing other religions into the mould formed by Christianity may well falsify their own nature.

This is a temptation when Christianity confronts other forms of monotheism particularly the great religions of Judaism and Islam. All three religions share some similarities. It could be said that they have faith in the same God as Creator of the universe and the God of Abraham. Even that will be disputed by Muslims who express belief in *one* God and not the three (Father, Son, and Holy Spirit) that they see Christians as worshipping. For similar reasons, Muslims would not think it right to have faith in Muhammad in the way that Christians profess faith in Christ. The Islamic view is that only God can be a proper object of faith, however much honour should be given to divine messengers. Any reference to faith in Christ is regarded as 'blasphemous mythology'.

Within Islam sincere belief in God, His books, angels, and so on has to mature into actions to become genuine faith (*iman*). The belief that faith implies must be validated by honourable works. Outward expression of inward, private faith must be demonstrated through practical observance, as enshrined in the law. St Paul's distrust, in his New Testament letters, of the primary role of law was directed at some contemporary Jewish understandings of law and its governance of human affairs even in minute matters. Christianity has always been vulnerable to the alternative objection that Paul himself faced that law can be totally discarded, because Christians had been freed from its shackles. The Christian stress on subjective faith may put greater emphasis on inward motivation than outward conformity to rules, but that points to the purpose of the rules, rather than just observing them for their own sake. Christ said that He came to fulfil divine law, not abolish it.

Jews and Muslims can part company from Christians in their stress on the centrality of law. One consequence has been the constant tension within Christianity between the idea of personal faith and that of external works. For Christianity, faith precedes action and gives it its point. Faith in Christ as Saviour can be crucial for Christian understandings, independently of the action it inspires. Although there are clear differences of emphasis between the religions, the contrast can be exaggerated. In the case of divergences between Christianity and Judaism, for example, it would be a mistake to suggest that, unlike Christianity, Jewish faith is so 'legalistic' that it is merely concerned with a mechanical observance of rules. While Christianity itself has at times seemed to become legalistic in that way, it should be remembered that the great injunction, commended by Jesus, to 'love the Lord your God with all your heart, and with all your soul and with all your might' was given in the Hebrew Bible in the book of Deuteronomy and was a foundation of Jewish law.

Even so, in Jewish and Islamic contexts, however important sincere belief might be, conformity to law as the expression of that belief is crucial. A Muslim theologian sums it up by saying: 'Islam is not a mystical faith of salvation wholly by external grace through a holy Saviour, human or divine, but rather a practical law-centred faith requiring human effort albeit aided by grace'. Islamic faith is constituted by obedience to God's laws, and particularly as revealed in *sharia* law. True faith, rather than mere belief, is only consolidated when it produces right action in accordance with that law. For that reason, Islam becomes a matter of faithfulness, and obedience, to the revealed will of God, rather than faith in a person such as Christ. The interpretation of that is of supreme importance, and Islam is a religion which stresses jurisprudence rather than speculative theology. The will of God can be known and followed through by working out the many implications for action implied by law as divinely revealed. Faithfulness to that law is the proper duty of a believer. This distinguishes Islamic faith from the Christian stress on the importance of faith as a personal relationship with God, as revealed in Christ. In this, Islam has followed the traditional Jewish respect for divine law (and its minutiae) that Christianity found problematic.

Another difference between Islamic ideas of faith (*iman*), and Christian notions is the implication that the Muslim believer should be certain of the truth of belief. Christian ideas of faith, however much they engender commitment, do not claim that kind of certainty. Christian faith is always regarded as a virtue which, like courage or temperance, cannot always be easily acquired and held to. Temptations and doubts have always been understood as obstacles to faith. That is why faith and hope have been coupled together as part of the traditional triad of faith, hope, and love seen as being at the heart of Christian life. We need not hope for what we are certain of.

In Islamic ethics, obedience to law provides merit in the sight of God. This stress on the role of law in serving God places religion firmly on the public stage. As we shall later see, laws are public and shared, and when faith is viewed as only being truly demonstrated in obedience to publicly enforced rules of conduct, it becomes significantly different from some versions of Christian faith that stress the role of individual commitment and belief. Even so, there is a tug in Christianity between the personal and the social, the private and the public. Both seem necessary counterparts to the other. Public behaviour needs private devotion and sincere commitment, while private faith is manifested in action. The old adage 'love God and do what you like' might be an invitation to cast off moral restraints, but a genuine love of God, it is asserted, should be reflected in a love of neighbour that results in definite beliefs about how people are to be treated. The difference with Islam may not always be in behaviour but in motivation. A personal faith in God could be the root of the one while obedience to divine revealed law is important for the other. An excessive stress on subjective faith can make that faith appear only of concern to its holder. In aspiring to truth, however, both Christianity and Islam make claims that purport to be of general application. They both aspire to the universality that this follows from the transcendence of the one God. Each maintains that that should be recognized by all people.

Scripture, reason, and tradition

Faith needs reason and understanding to focus on its object, while it seems that God must be revealed in concrete ways for humans to understand. Monotheism has needed its prophets who could point to God, but Christianity goes further by suggesting that God has literally come down to human level, through His Son becoming human, and demonstrating what God expects humans to be. Whatever might be said of this astounding claim, it provides a revelation of God in ways that humans can grasp. Through one human life, it gives content to faith, and its relevance to our life together. Christ, according to Christian faith, manifests the nature of God in human terms, while also showing what human life ought to be like.

There have, however, always been divergent claims within Christianity as well as between different religions, and the perennial issue has been how to settle such disputes. What criteria should be appealed to? Claims to divine revelation cannot be accepted at face value by any religion. There must be a continuing balance between faith and reason, even when humans reach out towards what appears to be inaccessible. In the 17th century, Locke explained: 'Whatever God has revealed is certainly true: no doubt can be made it. This is the proper object of faith, but whether it be a divine revelation or not, reason must judge.' Faith needs revelation but claims to revelation have to be tested even within the context of Christianity. Locke was all too aware in his own age of the danger of religious fanaticism. An ability to recognize genuine revelation may come from a reason that reflects the rationality of God, but that is still not proof. Despite his empiricist philosophy, Locke himself added the need for the guidance of Christian Scripture to that of reason.

The doctrine of justification by faith alone (*sola fide*) was particularly promulgated by Martin Luther at the Reformation as a challenge to the Roman Catholic Church's view of the authority of the Church through tradition. The Protestant emphasis gave a more immediate access for an individual to God and His revelation. There were dangers in the doctrine, as demonstrated by Locke's concerns. Individuals could become their own law-makers, with resulting civil strife and anarchy. Interpretation of Scripture needed guidance, without a return to blind obedience to Church hierarchy. The problem was balancing the individual conscience, and passionate faith, with rational and sober consideration.

A major influence on Locke was the 16th-century theologian and lawyer Richard Hooker, originally from Exeter. He wrote for the newly constituted Church of England, and set the foundation for a balanced approach for his Church. Even in Elizabethan times, Hooker was aware of the excesses of a 'Puritanism' that was already influential. He was concerned with the way stress on the supremacy of the Bible for faith could lead someone to interpret it by his or her 'own spirit'. Martin Luther had also given credence to the slogan *sola scriptura* ('by Scripture alone'). Hooker agreed that the Bible was our supreme source of knowledge of God's revelation, but he thought its interpretation should be guided. It may not mean what individuals at first sight imagine, with the result that different readers could take contradictory lessons from it. Hooker was the source of the lasting Anglican emphasis on the triad of reason, tradition, and Scripture, each acting as a check on the other. Scripture may remain silent about perfectly acceptable traditions, and tradition can pass on collective understandings of how certain passages should be interpreted. Reason too can play a restraining role, when confronted with wayward opinions depending on idiosyncratic views of parts of Scripture. Even so, Hooker believed that the Bible witnessed basic truths of divine revelation, and that the New Testament tells us how, in the Incarnation, God was revealed in Christ.

For Hooker, and the theology and philosophy he inspired, human reason was a result of a God-given faculty. He did not think that human understanding was too clouded by sin to be unable to grasp what was good and true. He even felt able to say that 'the general and perpetual voice of men is the witness of God himself'. Human reasoning could understand something of God before it received any direct revelation. Hooker confidently talked of the 'law of reason' in human nature and referred to the universal message of the Christian gospel. The Bible was not a proclamation for a particular group of people, but proclaimed a truth that all should recognize. Hooker's writings recognizably followed the pre-Reformation tradition of natural law and universal reason. Like the later Cambridge Platonists, he saw the crucial importance of human rationality as a gift of God and a path to partial knowledge of the divine. For example, natural reason, for Hooker, suggested that if we do not wish to suffer harm from others, we should not be prepared to inflict it. The commandment that we should love our neighbours as ourselves, he thought, finds an echo in our natural reasoning about what is right.

Hooker's view that God illuminates every person with the light of reason influenced his understanding of the place in society of the Christian Church, and the Church of England in particular. Truth for him was in principle accessible to everyone, even if only partially. What was true for the Church applied to those outside.

It was not a matter of being a member of the elect few, as Calvinists might suppose, nor the preserve of those who live by the Bible, important though that would be. Church and society should be concerned with the same issues, using the same reason. The Church should not regard itself as totally separate from the rest of society. Its witness applied to all and there were grounds for expecting the Church also to listen to those beyond its doors. Clearly this bolstered the claims of an Established Church to play a full part in society. Faith and society operated in a common domain. Truth was not the preserve of people of faith, because a rationality open to all called attention to a truth of universal relevance.

Hooker followed his mediaeval predecessors in thinking that reason was compatible with ideas of the supernatural and transcendent. The Bible pointed to a realm beyond, and it was no part of reason to rule it out. Even so, the triad of reason, Scripture, and tradition does raise tensions, when the different elements pull in different directions. At the Reformation, appeal to Scripture posed questions about some of the traditions of the Roman Catholic Church. The demands of reason, at least as narrowly defined, can be made to appear to contradict the assertions of Scripture. How are divergences to be resolved? Hooker and his Anglican successors wanted all three parts to pull in the same direction, believing that, otherwise, something is going wrong.

While some accept that Christian faith is exclusively based on the Bible, others look for supporting evidence. One dilemma is whether the contents of the Bible are true because they are in the Bible, or whether they are in the Bible because they are true. If the latter, truth might also be partly accessible through tradition and reason. As Hooker feared, narrowing matters to what the Bible appears to say to an individual can result in a vicious subjectivism. Divergent interpretations will be unchecked by other means. The contrary danger, as the Enlightenment later demonstrated, was that fashionable views of reason could dismiss any alleged divine revelation. Being open to wider society, and its understandings, has also brought the danger (always a temptation for an Established Church) of allowing prevalent fads and fashions to modify core Christian doctrine to fit the spirit of the passing age.

The Bible was seen as important because of the revelation it bears witness to, although, often regarded as 'Holy Writ', it could never play the same part in the life of Christians that the Qu'ran plays in Islam. The latter is seen as directly emanating from God, or Allah, while for most Christians the Bible just witnesses to the truth. Another way of putting the point, perhaps more provocatively, is that the Bible is not itself the Word of God, because it witnesses to that Word, the *logos*, as revealed in Christ.

Hooker was an influential thinker in the early days of the Church of England. Continuing with earlier notions of natural law, the law of reason written on human hearts, he tried to provide a balance that restrained the wilder enthusiasms of Puritans, while still standing by what he saw as the truths of the Christian gospel. In addition to the dangers of deferring to the current opinions of a particular generation, there was another issue. Stressing truth for everyone, not just the Church, may be crucial for ideas of the Church's role and mission, but a faith that recognizes truth and does not act on it is useless. Arguments about the relevant contributions of the triad, Scripture, reason, and tradition, could become detached from the question about how far faith should make a difference to people's lives. If the Christian proclamation is true, it has to affect people. Arguments about truth and its sources cannot become mere intellectual puzzles, or degenerate into battles for power within the Church, for instance between laity and bishops.

An absorption with rationality produced at times a dry and intellectual faith that often left the Anglican Church in the 18th century unrelated to society and its needs. This was eventually addressed both in England and in the American colonies, such as Anglican Virginia, by the Evangelical Revival, and John Wesley's Methodism in particular. Religion then made a greater impact on people's lived experience. It was in that spirit, particularly in the American United Methodist Church, that a fourth element was added to the triad, namely experience, to form what was known as the 'Wesleyan quadrilateral'. Whatever the validity of that fourth element, it reinforced the relevance of faith to personal commitment and ensuing action. That will be a recurring theme.

The challenge of religious disagreement

If reason plays a part in faith, not least in specifying what the faith is about, there remains the problem that there is disagreement within religions, between religions, and about all religion. Accepting beliefs that others reject may seem problematic if one wishes to be rational. When anyone claims to see an elephant in a field, the fact that others disagree should make us pause, and investigate further. Perhaps one person has a better view than the others, or they do not know what an elephant is. Even so, such disagreement can make some judgements seem risky. Assuming we are all what has been called by contemporary philosophers 'epistemic peers', with an equal ability to see what is the case, we cannot all be in a privileged position to gain knowledge of what is true. If we disagree about whether there is an elephant in front of us, the rational implication is that one of us at least must be wrong. It may be difficult to determine who that is.

Ordinary disagreements should in principle be resolvable. In science, there are generally recognized procedures for settling empirical disputes, but there can be irreconcilable disputes even among scientists. They can occur particularly when information might in principle be limited, as in arguments about the origins of the universe. In religion, on the other hand, religious disagreement ordinarily seems much more intractable. Talking of 'religious diversity' suggests that truth may not be at stake and we are merely at odds concerning different 'faiths', not about something that can be rationally resolved.

In everyday life, when faced with indeterminate objects, perhaps in a thick fog, it might be right to suspend judgement in the face of disagreement. That could in the case of religion encourage people in roughly similar positions, but making different decisions, to adopt an agnostic position, and suspend judgement. Indeed, those who are sure of their atheism may have as much reason to doubt their own position as any religious believers standing by their faith. In each case, apparently rational people facing the same claims come to different conclusions. Each might conclude on that basis there is no reliable basis for either set of beliefs.

The problem is that this kind of reasoning can be applied to any case of apparently irresolvable disagreement. There may be occasions when it is right to defer to people judged more expert than oneself, for instance in the field of medicine. That is where the idea of epistemological peers becomes relevant, because experts, by definition, know more than others do. What, though, should happen when experts in the same field disagree? Philosophy is itself notorious as a source of disagreements between people of seemingly similar expertise. Is rationality itself challenged when disagreements continue? If so, it appears that philosophy at the highest level becomes irrational, or encourages a refusal to commit to any view. That is the route to paralysis, and at some point, in any context, we all have to act in accordance with one belief rather than another.

Once a particular faith, especially a religious one, is challenged because it is not shared by all of one's intellectual peers, however defined, we might doubt our own views. That is when the idea of faith becomes relevant. I must continue to trust my own judgement and out of faith hope that I am right. Otherwise all disagreement about complex matters, not only in religion but in philosophy, morality, politics, and even at the frontiers of science, will make everyone subject to debilitating doubt. Faith then involves not being too easily swayed by the opinions of others when they are different to ours. We may continue to question and listen to others but we cannot just give up and opt out of taking any stance to the world. None of us is omniscient, and all still have to make decisions, and live by them. This may engender humility but should not leave us in despair. The search for truth is more important than the comfort of conformity.

Apart from the basic disagreement between theist and atheist, other levels of divergence emerge, both within and between religions. Different religions attest to different alleged divine revelations. Even within a particular religion, even the major monotheistic ones, there are significant differences. Some might wish to rely on apparent experts, such as an *ayatollah* or a pope, but that involves recognizing that they are what they claim to be. The authority of different Scriptures such as the Bible or the Qu'ran can also be challenged, and both are interpreted in diverse ways. Disagreements about the worth of any religious faith, questions about which religion can be true, and issues about particular doctrines within a religion are all difficult to resolve. The lack of unity within different divisions of the Christian Church is well documented. Other religions also contain many internal disputes, such as between liberal and Orthodox Judaism, or Sunni and Shia in Islam.

Bewildering diversity might be a convincing argument against the rationality of holding any religious faith. Can religious faith itself claim to involve rational beliefs when it spawns such disagreement? One problem in the face of apparent disagreement is how to regard our opponents. If we respect them and recognize their rationality, that might make us question and doubt our own beliefs. If we claim insights that others do not have, we may appear to be claiming to be more rational than them in an arrogant fashion. At what stage can so-called 'epistemic humility', and acceptance of our limitations, shade into doubt and the wavering of faith? A willingness to discuss rational difficulties for our religious belief, particularly with unbelievers, might seem an admission of doubt, and evidence of weak faith. Religious faith typically demands obedience and loyalty to the object of worship, namely God. Unbelievers are under no such constraint and may feel they can be open-minded because apparently they have no faith to lose.

This argument can produce an opposite conclusion. When believers are unwilling to argue about the truth of their beliefs and defend them, this could indicate disloyalty to God, because of a lurking fear that beliefs about God are in the last resort indefensible. Those who are confident that their faith is focused on truth should perhaps in all consistency expose themselves to rational criticism and scrutiny. Those who genuinely believe that God is the source of truth should be willing to follow arguments to wherever the truth lies. There, a religious believer would hold, God will still be found. The question of the possibility of an objective truth that is independent of all particular beliefs, draws us into metaphysics and the possibility of some ultimate grounding for what is true. Many philosophers have traditionally believed that it is grounded in theism, so that the ideas of God and of truth are ultimately inseparable. If so, seekers after truth need never fear the conclusion of arguments about the truth of religious beliefs. As we have seen, even the 19th-century philosopher, Nietzsche, saw truth and God as inseparable, but claimed that 'God is dead'. His repudiation of any notion of objective truth seemed the only possible logical conclusion.

One option, in the face of widespread disagreement, is to seek majority opinion, but that raises the issue of which majority. This comes back to the question of 'epistemic peers' and who they are. Do we look for the opinion of all humans, all our contemporaries, those of equal education, or what? Including the opinion of our ancestors is to give weight to tradition, as many religious people

47

would. The problem is that we find ourselves in a circular argument, so that the majority we choose is one that agrees with us. Another issue is that looking at what people believe changes the subject from where the truth lies to what people think about it. Rationality, as a guide to truth, should not be defined in terms of consensus and agreement. Majorities have often in the history of the world proved very wrong. Faith may not be less rational because it cannot command general agreement. In the development of science, one person has sometimes initially had an access to some truth denied others. That is true in religions where insights seem to have been conveyed because of a special revelation to one person and others then coming to accept them.

Religious faith is often criticized because it appeals to factors that may not be publicly recognized. That brings us back to the question of what happens to be generally agreed at a particular time, and religion is not the only area where there is much controversy and major disagreements. Politics and ethics provide other such examples, and like religion are particularly concerned with human life and collide with issues about self-interest. Perhaps Nietzsche was right and the will to power underlies everything. Perhaps religion is just an example of where different groups and social organizations try to control each other. The problem is that this destroys the idea of reason, and any possibility of living together peaceably while disagreeing even about fundamental matters.

Chapter 4
Faith and science

Science and progress

The 18th-century Enlightenment in France deified reason at the expense of religious faith, which was seen as the product of superstition. Faith in anything beyond the reach of human reason was derided once human autonomy and rationality were made supreme. It appeared to be the instrument of an oppressive institution, *l'ancien régime*, in which the Roman Catholic Church held a prominent position. What justified this faith in reason? We must all stand somewhere and have agreed starting points for reasoning. Humans cannot always question everything. The question is how to find a basis for agreement about the character of a constantly changing world and our place in it.

The 18th century was a time of optimism, with talk of progress, of the growth of knowledge, and of 'improvement'. Increased knowledge could give more control over the conditions of human life, so that things, it seemed, could only get better. Ignorance alone, it was felt, held people back. Everyone was assumed to be essentially good, and lack of knowledge could be the only impediment. Faith in another, inaccessible world seemed irrelevant.

Belief in progress has been put into doubt by the experiences of the 20th century. Knowledge seemed to produce more efficient methods of mass extermination, whether through gas ovens or nuclear bombs. Even so, many in the 21st century hold to the same gospel of hope and progress, believing that humans not only could improve morally, but are improving morally. The Harvard psychologist, Steven Pinker, voices a widespread view when he champions such Enlightenment principles. For him, the ideas of reason, science, humanism, and progress are all welded together. Despite discouraging historical precedents, he believes that humans are improving conditions of life for everyone and will continue to improve them. He invokes 'the Enlightenment belief that by understanding the world we can improve the human condition'.

Pinker sees religion as an enemy of this improvement. He claims: 'To take something on faith means to believe it without good reason, so by definition a faith in the existence of supernatural entities clashes with reason.' At the core, Pinker holds that 'the scientific facts militate towards a defensible morality, namely principles that maximise the flourishing of humans and other sentient beings'. Can, though, scientific knowledge give us guidance about what matters or is worthwhile, or tell us what it is to flourish? It can instruct us how to get what we want, but not what we ought to want. The discoveries of science can be used well or badly. Technological advances have brought about climate change, pollution, and many threats to human health. Science has not shown itself very adept at setting priorities or deciding what is most crucial for human welfare. It can do great good, particularly in the field of medicine, but human beings must still make judgements about how best to apply its insights. Because something can be done, does not mean it has to be done, or even ought to be. The 18th-century empiricist philosopher, David Hume, underestimated the potential of human reason. He famously maintained that reason is 'the slave of the passions'. However it should be capable not just of calculating the best means to desired ends but of estimating how desirable those ends should be. In his book on *Rationality*, Pinker suggests that 'pursuing our goals and desires is not the opposite of reason but ultimately the reason we have reason'. A more generous view of reason could also recognize its capability of seeing what is true, in a way that can guide us. It can show us what our goals and desires ought to be, and help mould and change them.

The idea of humanism, with its stress on the centrality of humans in any scheme of things, as well, perhaps, as their basic goodness, is itself controversial. Why do all human beings matter? Why should we care for those who cannot reciprocate? Are people more important than animals? Should animal interests be sacrificed for the greater good of humans? Many now think that some non-human animals have moral standing, and this view is itself seen as a sign of progress. Contemporary science may appear to blur distinctions between humans and animals, but others conclude that if animals are to be treated like human beings, it is likely that human beings may become treated like animals. The point is not to answer these questions but to suggest that reference to scientific progress does little to answer them. Morality needs a wider understanding of humanity's place in the world. Any vision that places science at the epicentre cannot explain why humans, or indeed animals, are of any importance. We are all, it seems, lumps of matter like any other physical object.

Such total commitment to science, and belief in its capacity to improve the lot of humanity, goes beyond available evidence. It involves a leap of faith as great as any religious position. It faces countervailing evidence of continuing widespread cruelty and persecution. It ignores genocide, wars, including civil wars, and general widespread indifference to the welfare of others. Belief in inevitable progress, including moral progress, is uplifting, and a motive for action. Yet it is not obvious that the world works that way, and in so far as that belief goes beyond available evidence it too rests on a form of faith.

The nature of science

Science claims universality in practice as well as theory. Scientists say that, while one can refer to different philosophies, European, Anglo-American, Chinese, and so on, science is not like that. There is one science, and experimental results in Beijing must be valid in Washington, DC. There is one world, and the science that attempts to investigate its nature cannot break up into separate squabbling units, although they can look at different aspects of the same world. The unity of science is important, and its agreed methods seem to set a standard for rationality, giving a route to agreement across cultures. It is often pointed out that, despite their claims to universal truth, different religions fail to agree and do not seem to know how to set about finding agreement.

Trust in scientific method as the final arbiter of all truth is still often taken as part of the definition of what it is to be rational in any sphere. The influence of a rigid empiricism, and even logical positivism, lives on, particularly in academic circles beyond philosophy. In his *Rationality*, Pinker, as a psychologist, alleges that 'Western religious belief is safely parked in the mythology zone', on the grounds that 'belief in God is an idea that falls outside the sphere of testable reality'. God's existence cannot, it is surmised, be considered 'a matter of truth or falsity'. Reason cannot get a grip on the belief. This attitude extends into many other disciplines, many of them influencing the way we share a common life. A philosopher of law, Brian Leiter, deals with the issue of how far contemporary law in Western nations should respect religious faith. He says of the major religious traditions: 'All countenance at least some central beliefs that are not ultimately answerable to evidence and reason as these are understood elsewhere (e.g. in common sense and science)'. He stresses that 'the distinctively religious state of mind is that of faith—that is of believing something notwithstanding the evidence of reasons that fail to support it, or even contradict it.' That sums up a common view even beyond the bounds of scientific practice. Reason and evidence are defined in narrowly scientific terms, and religious faith is considered irrational.

'Science' is not a monolithic enterprise. Its different disciplines concentrate on different facets of the physical world, and sometimes can be difficult to combine. Should the findings of biology ultimately be reducible to those of physics, or those of psychology to the workings of the brain? Are the social sciences properly scientific? Is economics a science in the way physics is? Maybe there are different levels of reality, to be investigated separately, or perhaps everything can ultimately be explained in the language of basic physics. These philosophical questions ask whether it is meaningful to talk of 'science' without specifying which branch of science, and which aspect of the world it is looking at. Different branches of science, such as biological sciences and the behavioural sciences, may suggest different possibilities. What is relevant may be a matter of rational judgement, but that itself comes from outside the narrow bounds of experimental science.

The simplification of 'science', and its associated worldview, can encourage a straight contrast with 'religion', itself a concept with many facets. The title of a book on science and religion by a geneticist, Jerry Coyne, says it all, *Faith versus Facts*. He articulates the common attitude that 'science' as a whole deals with 'facts', and they are defined in distinction from whatever faith might be. The author characterizes trust in faith as 'fideism', a vice of which he imagines science is free, as it does not involve 'faith'. He defines fideism as the view that faith and reason are incompatible, and in fact 'mutually hostile'. Of course, when science defines what is to be factual, it will exclude religion, but it is a circular argument as it justifies science in terms set by science.

St Paul, together with the early Christian theologians, Coyne provocatively says, 'were unremitting in their attacks on reason'.

St Paul, however, came from Tarsus, a major centre of ancient philosophy, was well versed in Greek philosophy, and knew how rational argument would appeal to the Greek and Roman worlds of the time. He was explicit at the beginning of his Epistle to the Romans that a belief in God as Creator was a matter of rationally understanding 'His power and deity' in part 'through the things God has made'. Knowledge of God should be clear for all humans because God has revealed it to them. In that, St Paul marked out the territory of natural theology, and the ability of the human mind to have some conception of God from looking at the physical world. Paul stressed in his preaching the special revelation of God through Christ, but for him faith still builds on reason, and its claims to universality.

Natural theology was the basis for the development of science with its assumptions about the regularity of the world. Laws of nature were thought to be derived from a law-making God. Modern science still depends on assumptions about the regularity and order inherent in the physical world, although many scientists ignore how they might be justified. Even if humans may live in an orderly world, why should that be true of the whole 'cosmos'? That word, an ancient Greek one, implies something arranged and ordered, as in 'cosmetic'. Assuming basic regularities throughout the physical world enables science to predict what will happen elsewhere or in the future. Without an ability to generalize, to go from here to there or now to then, the practice of science becomes impossible.

Coyne is typical of many, both within science and beyond, in resisting any attempt to give a rational basis for science or accepting that science itself involves any kind of faith. He contrasts a faith that the sun will rise tomorrow because it always has, with a religious belief which, however confident, 'is not based on evidence sufficient to command assent from any reasonable person'. Yet reducing the idea of evidence to what is now scientifically available puts blinkers on science. What can now be counted as evidence can reflect human limitations as much as the nature of what is being investigated. When scientists claim, 'there is no evidence that the virus is spreading', many may conclude that the virus is not spreading. Yet the absence of available evidence may be a sign of current ignorance. Claims to scientific knowledge are always tentative and provisional, and must be subject to revision. Scientists decide what is to count as relevant evidence because of the theories they hold, and those theories cannot be mere deductions from 'sense data' ('given' through the experience), a view that has been derided as 'the bucket theory of the mind'. Scientists are not passive recipients of information, but active participants in the scientific endeavour, with some preconceived idea, or theory, of what might be important.

Theory and facts

A catalyst for a new understanding of the way science works, which is still influential, was the work of Thomas S. Kuhn. With his emphasis on scientific 'paradigms', or alternative rule-governed patterns of research, his book *The Structure of Scientific Revolutions* in 1962 was highly significant for the philosophy of science. He distinguished between normal science and revolutionary science when sudden change brought about a new way of seeing the world. After a scientific revolution, such as the change from classical to quantum mechanics, everything looks different. Kuhn drew an analogy with experiments in psychology where the same picture can be interpreted differently. The familiar example of a duck-rabbit, mentioned by Kuhn, was also used by Wittgenstein, in an implied criticism of the empiricist idea of raw sense data that we passively receive. The same drawing can be seen either as a duck with a beak looking one way, or as a rabbit with floppy ears looking in the opposite direction. The question, which for Wittgenstein was unanswerable, was whether in both cases we interpret the same image, the same data, differently, or whether each perception is itself different with its own meaning. Expectations, theory, and interpretation have active roles to play,

55

not just in how we understand the world, but perhaps in how we experience it in the first place.

For Kuhn, a new paradigm means that the world the scientist now experiences will seem 'incommensurable' with the previous one. The two cannot be compared. What is real depends so much on the nature of a particular theory that Kuhn was able to assert that 'after a revolution scientists work in a different world'. In parallel manner, the British philosopher of religion writing in the latter part of the last century, John Hick, talks of how religious and non-religious minds experience the same situation differently because they interpret it in fundamentally different ways, although he would not himself have talked of 'different worlds'. He significantly says: 'I identify this voluntary interpretive element within our conscious experience as faith.' He follows this by claiming that our ordinary, natural experience of the world 'is as much a matter of faith as the religious; for all our conscious experience is experiencing-as'. Religious faith can then seem like the alleged faith lying at the root of ordinary experience of our common world. Too much stress on active understanding takes us away from thinking that we confront an independent and objective world, with which we come to terms. Instead of discovering the nature of 'the world', we are then understood to construct our own particular world, whoever 'we' happen to be. The invocation of personal faith can encourage subjectivism or relativism, so that truth depends on who is recognizing it. Scientists will then live in a world created by their current theory, and a religious person 'of faith' will be in a different world from those of the atheist, or of believers in different religions. Each sees things differently, and there appears nothing beyond their faith to which they can appeal.

Kuhn's views made major changes in science into leaps of faith, and a faith defined in its own terms, rather than by what it appears to be about. He set science on a path towards the post-modern idea that science is one social practice amongst many, without any claim to universality. However, the question of justification can never disappear. Why accept science if it cannot appeal to firm foundations? One well-known philosopher of science, Imre Lakatos, even in the late 1960s interpreted Kuhn as saying that 'there is no way of judging the theory but by accessing the number, faith and vocal energy of its supporters'. That could only mean that truth is the product of power, itself a view with many contemporary resonances more than half a century later.

Post-modernist views, defining themselves against the Enlightenment view of universal reason, dethrone science, so that it itself becomes the product of 'mere' faith. Even in science, different theories will fight it out with no rational way of deciding between them. Kuhn drew a religious parallel, by saying that 'the transfer of allegiance from paradigms is a conversion experience that cannot be forced'. His pessimistic conclusion was that total conversion to the new paradigms takes time. Older scientists will be stubborn and set in their ways. He adds: 'Conversions will occur a few at a time until, after the last holdouts have died, the whole profession will again be practising under a single, but now a different, paradigm.'

The thought underlying all this is that, even within science, the switch from one way of looking at the world to another, from one paradigm to another, depends on psychological and social causes but not reason. Truth is then constituted by what people think, rather than what they think about. Kuhn started down the path that leads to relativism, even scepticism, about truth, so that scientific theories just reflect the kind of people constructing them.

Justifying science

Whereas the 18th-century Enlightenment saw itself as challenging authority, guided by the pure light of reason, appeals to rationality and even science itself can be seen as techniques that merely amplify the influence of certain groups. References to 'faith' and 'conversion' can imply a derogatory view of religious faith as an arbitrary commitment. Conversion can be seen in the same light as 'indoctrination' in education. Such comparisons with religious faith are possible because it has already been denigrated. Some dismiss any philosophical quest for the rational basis of science by insisting that 'science works'. Yet the idea that the results of science alone justify its 'usefulness' makes science a self-justifying enterprise. It becomes oblivious to questions about the ethics of what it might be doing, or to any other external standards of rationality.

The view that science can explain everything in its own terms has been dubbed 'scientism'. It exhibits a blind trust in the methods of science, wherever they might take us. If public policy is to be 'evidence led', and if contemporary science defines what is to count as evidence, we are in a parlous position. In fact, science as it now is will change over the years, and we must be aware of its deficiencies as well as its strengths. For example, in any new situation such as a pandemic, required data may not be immediately available. Initial leaps of imagination in thinking of how to deal with the situation may be necessary, and these could be seen as acts of faith, which may or may not turn out to be justified.

No-one should rely on blind faith, or arbitrary commitment. The human power of rationality enables everyone to examine alternatives and choose reasons, which can themselves be challenged. Such reasons, however, are rarely strong enough to 'prove' something beyond all doubt. Rationality is not just possessed by those I agree with, and dialogue and attempts at mutual understanding can be a path to further knowledge. Criticisms may even help me to understand my own beliefs better. Even within science, all are prone to error, and liable to follow their own advantage. Faith in anything needs grounded belief. We may not have a logical proof or complete empirical evidence, but we need reasons that suggest we are going in the right direction. Even the idea of evidence must not be reduced to what 'science' can currently acknowledge. Its practice needs rational justification that does not appeal, in a circular manner, to its own contemporary assumptions.

This goes against some contemporary theories of meaning such as that stemming from the later Wittgenstein. Reacting against rigid scientistic views, he accepted different uses of language in their own terms. He looked for meaning within different social contexts, instead of assuming, as he once had, that language just referred to something external. He was not unlike the American pragmatists in affirming the manner in which beliefs were embedded in different practices and forms of life. He alleged that we cannot justify basic beliefs such as the existence of the earth by appealing to some reality independent of our concepts. He says that it is 'rather a part of the whole *picture* which forms the starting point of belief for me'. Significantly, 'picture' is precisely the word that he uses to describe the views entertained by those with religious belief, such as that of the Last Judgement. Science was not regarded as being in some way superior to religion, just different, as, say, one game is different from another with different rules. There are different 'language-games', each with different rules of what is acceptable.

The inadequacy of this way of thinking is accidentally illustrated by an example Wittgenstein himself gave, in 1950. He refused to accept that someone had been on the moon, not because at the time it happened to be false, but because, as he put it, 'our whole system of physics forbids us to believe it'. Within twenty years, it happened, and even in 1950 had been foreseeable. Reality had the last word. The world that science tries to understand, like the transcendent reality reached for in religion, is not an arbitrary construction, or a picture of the world. It either exists or it does not, and theories and beliefs have to be able to account for its characteristics.

Significantly, Wittgenstein immediately follows the example of travel to the moon with a remark about religion. He says that the denial that people can get to the moon is like the way 'one can instruct the child to believe in a God, or that none exists, and it will accordingly be able to produce apparently telling grounds for the one or the other'. He treats both religion and physics in the same way, as the product of indoctrination. The Enlightenment idea of rationality claiming universal validity is rejected. Players of different language-games become warring factions without common ground for dialogue. Non-participants in a system of faith, or language-game, religious or not, will find much of what is going on incomprehensible, much as a fan of cricket will find the manoeuvres of American football impenetrable, and vice versa.

Rational justification reaches beyond social environments. Science is no more self-authenticating than religious faith. It is not enough that an identifiable group of people subscribe collectively to its methods, because in all aspects of human life, we face a reality that we discover but do not construct. The work of Kuhn and Wittgenstein moved attention from the justification of beliefs to their social context. 'Paradigms', 'theories', 'systems', and 'language-games' each involve shared activities and beliefs. This turn to sociology, instead of rational justification, was a reaction to a scientism that claimed exclusive rights to knowledge. Knowledge was seen as socially constructed, and the so-called 'sociology of knowledge' became influential towards the end of the 20th century. Trusting the efficacy of sociology, though, as an avenue to truth relies on faith in something beyond the discipline and its practices. Like other areas of would-be science, it assumes a reality beyond its own projections, in this case that of social structures, seen as causally influencing individuals, their beliefs, and behaviour. The context in which all science, including social science, can operate still involves trust in reason, and appeals, sometimes implicit, to truth.

When, though, we talk of rational justification in the context of faith, we must be careful. Fideism sees faith as justified in its own terms and repudiates any idea that it should be subservient to the demands of reason. Opponents question the idea that religious faith must be justified by that faith alone, but this carries with it the seeds of confusion. It seems to call into play the Protestant doctrine of 'justification by faith'. That all faith may need rational justification, however partial, is a different issue from the theological doctrine of justification by faith. The doctrine does not mean that faith is self-justifying, and contrasts not faith and reason, but faith and works. It deals with the separate issue of personal 'salvation', of how an individual is put right, or exonerated, in God's eyes. The argument has been that humans could not earn God's favour by their own efforts. We do not build up capital to pay for entry to heaven. The form of justification invoked is more like a defence in a court of law than the rational establishment of truth. It justifies a person not an idea. Juxtaposing faith and works deals with questions of individual worth and merit. It raises the connection between faith and moral behaviour, to which we now turn.

Chapter 5
Faith and morality

Merit and grace

Religious faith is not just an answer to an intellectual puzzle, but usually functions as a guide to life. Such faith involves the 'heart' as well as the head, and demands a commitment that makes a radical difference to how a life is lived. That could mean that we concentrate on action rather than the content of belief, on morality rather than the promptings of our minds. Faith then becomes just a moral stance. For the theologian, faith without works has often seemed barren, and it is not surprising that in modern Christian theology much energy has been spent on this question. The twin commandments at the root of Christian belief are to love God and to love your neighbour. What is the connection between the two? Can you truly love God, when you do not love your neighbour, or is love of God to be expressed simply in terms of loving your neighbour? The former seems highly abstract, and stress on a so-called 'social gospel' maintained that genuine faith should be more concerned with social justice than private belief. That moved the focus from individual to collective action, and even replaced morality with politics.

Faith has usually started with the individual. Christianity has typically stressed personal accountability to God, and individual responsibility. A famous passage in St Paul's Letter to the

Ephesians proclaims: 'By grace are you saved through faith, and that not of your own doing, as it is the gift of God. It is not the result of your own deeds, so that no-one may boast.' The question then arises whether, if faith is the result of God's action, I can be held responsible for it at all. Am I just putty in God's hands? There have been times in Christian theology (for instance, in Calvinism after the Reformation) when the idea of faith as a gift of 'grace' has produced the idea that God has especially chosen some people, 'the elect', rather than others. The universal applicability of the Christian Gospel has at times been put in question.

St Thomas Aquinas commented that two things are requisite for faith, saying: 'First, the things which are of faith shall be proposed to man...The second is the assent of the believer for the things proposed to him.' The content of faith is presented to us, when we open our hearts and minds to its possibility. That is like saying that the world around us is presented to us when we open our eyes and look. In the case of faith, we must also accept the consequences of seeing, and live our life accordingly. Personal accountability is important, and Christian theology recognizes that we are accountable for our response, if not the content of faith presented. Our ideas of God may be made possible by divine action, but we ourselves determine how to react.

The grace of God is said to be demonstrated in His willingness to approach us. Our willingness to be open to that, and to respond, is said to matter eternally. Faith, it is taught, needs an acknowledgement of total dependence on God. It cannot glory in its own achievements or be self-reliant. We may be accountable, but we do not earn God's grace, it is thought. The problem is that a sense of personal responsibility can degenerate into pride, so that we think we gain merit through our response, instead of humbly accepting our own unworthiness. People who prosper can then appear to have earned God's favour, while those suffering misfortune may seem to have deserved it. Both attitudes can, it seems, enter into views of faith in God. The idea that through our faith, and actions, we can 'bend God's grace in our favour', as the political philosopher Michael Sandel puts it, can be insidious. He points out that 'the secular version of this idea made for an exhilarating promise of individual freedom' so that 'we can imagine our fate is in our hands and that those who do well in this life, do so because they deserve to'. The wealthy not only assume that they have earned their comfort, but that the needy too have got what they deserve. The modern idea of meritocracy is born.

Christianity has stressed the importance of freedom, and its concomitant responsibilities, but in a way that should not degenerate into pride, or a lack of humility. These are out of place in the context of divine judgement. Once such ideas of freedom become detached from the faith to which they were bound, in Sandel's words, 'merit tends to drive out grace'. When actions are separated from faith, success becomes a personal achievement. Self-satisfaction replaces gratitude. This may not be part of a Christian idea of faith, but such ideas gain currency in a secularizing society. Faith may be a gift, but we are responsible for its effects. What we decide to do matters, but if we consider that we deserve a reward for what we are doing, our faith is centred on ourselves and not what is transcendent. Pride destroys true faith, or so Christian teaching would have us believe.

Individual and community

Personal faith may degenerate into an idea of merit, and that is certainly in tune with modern ideas about the autonomy of the individual. Those may owe their origin to religious, particularly Protestant, beliefs about individual accountability before God. 'Faith' though, as we have seen, can refer to corporate belief, as in reference to 'faith communities'. The tug between faith as an individual achievement and as collective possession is reflected in the venerable dispute arising from Protestantism as to whether churches are voluntary associations of committed individuals, or whether there is, as Roman Catholics, in particular, would have it, one Church, as the organic body of Christ on earth, collectively deciding, and teaching, what proper faith consists in. The tension between individual and collective, personal and social, can become an argument about the proper meaning of faith. The Roman Catholic Church refers to its flock collectively as 'the faithful'. It is not always individual commitments that are being invoked, but their membership of a community, defined in particular by baptism.

Protestantism has often focused more on individual commitment, while the Roman Catholic Church has sometimes emphasized the social dimension, with people seen as above all members of a community. This echoes wider controversies. At times, individual consciences have clashed with the authority of the Church, and concern about where the weight of Christian teaching should be. Is a quest for personal holiness the spur to social action, or an obstacle to it? What is the relationship between personal morality, and political action? Whether faith is an individual concern or the property of a community, and whether it is a matter of belief and doctrine, or 'works' and social action, have been questions about the meaning and purpose of Christian faith. It can sink into a subjectivism, regarded as valid only for an individual, or it could be regarded as the property of a community, such as 'the' Church, and that can degenerate into the relativism that only sees faith as 'its truth'.

The issues of belief and practice, and individual and community, cannot be separated. All four components are part of any religious faith, particularly that of the monotheistic religions. Different religious strands carry different stresses, but sometimes with the loss of important elements. To take faith as a wholly individual matter neglects the crucial question of how any faith and doctrine can be shared, or passed on through generations. Even voluntary associations need continuing structures if they are not to dwindle and die out when individual enthusiasms wane. The Roman Catholic Church has a 'magisterium' to control the content of faith, with authority to declare what is heretical. In the case of morality, the individual might be expected to live according to the collective will of the institution. The Protestant stress on the centrality of the individual conscience increases the idea of personal responsibility. That, in turn, can degenerate into people becoming a law unto themselves, losing sight of what is objectively right or wrong. Whatever the emphasis, both individuals and institutions confront the same reality, and must appreciate that issues of truth are independent of all their beliefs and activities.

Religious education

The question of social structures raises the issue of education. How does one ensure that children are taught what is seen as true, so that they are protected from harm and taught how to treat others properly? Religious and moral views appear inextricably linked. In a radically pluralist society, people cannot agree where truth might lie, and there will be disagreement about what should be taught. Some evade the issue by merely wanting to teach children how to be 'autonomous' and make up their own minds, but parents wish to pass on their own religious faith and its implications for behaviour to their children. That is not a subject for rational debate when faith is only of subjective concern, but if a religious faith involves pretensions to be a true claim to truth, it becomes a matter of public debate. If education is to be a prerogative of the State, and publicly funded, should the State determine the content of education? When there was a settled Christian consensus in England, it was easy for the State to provide an education based on broadly Christian assumptions, with daily worship and teaching about the Bible on a non-denominational basis. That is no longer the case.

Any State is still confronted with the strong desire of many parents for their children to be educated according to the moral principles of their various faiths, even when they run counter to current social trends. In England there are Anglican and Roman

Catholic schools, as well as publicly funded schools for others, such as Muslims and Jews. Some lobbyists object to any such segregated education, but so-called 'faith schools' were often built by the Churches themselves, the Church of England and other denominations, before there was any national provision for free education. They have always served the wider community, as well as adherents of their own faith.

There are problems both for the consciences of parents and for public policy. Should parents allow their children to be exposed to teaching they would regard as harmful, particularly in morality? Should the State override the wishes of parents in pursuit of public policy? An education based largely on the study of holy texts, as some Orthodox Jewish and Muslim schools would wish, might be too narrow, and squeeze out a more general education. In an English-speaking country, for instance, teaching English language might appear essential. There have been American court cases in New York State, for example, about the education of Orthodox Jews in 'yeshivas', special schools where most of the school day is spent studying the canon of Jewish texts, particularly the Torah and the Talmud. Any government might consider it has a duty to ensure a broader education for all its students. Should parents have the right to educate their children privately, removing them from the secular influences of a State school? Parental rights are enshrined in human rights law. The 1948 United Nations Declaration of Human Rights, drawn up in the shadow of Nazi indoctrination, asserts that 'parents have a prior right to choose the kind of education that should be given to their children'.

Some countries wish to prohibit home-schooling, with the idea that national values independent of religious faith must be inculcated. In Germany, some children have, at least for a time, been removed from parents refusing to send their children to a State school. The courts upheld the view that State regulation was necessary in a democratic society, to encourage pluralism. Any

State should have to protect a child in the child's own interests, in cases of flagrant abuse. That does not settle what should happen when sincere parental judgements about what is beneficial or harmful to the child are at odds with the judgement of the State. This becomes crucial in avowedly secular States, not rooted in any religious faith. A failure to integrate children into society can appear to threaten the emergence of parallel societies and the collapse of social cohesion. France stresses 'republican values'. There is talk of 'British values' in the same context. At the extreme, a totalitarian society can try to bend the wills of children to obey its own interests, using education as its instrument.

Religious parents want to teach their children their own beliefs. Religious institutions wish to teach, and preach, if possible, through ordinary processes of education. Yet once faith is seen as private, it has to be excluded from public education. That though, in a democracy, presupposes a consensus about what is important for public life. Choices concerning religion should still be informed ones. The problems of 'religious illiteracy' have become commonplace in Western societies. Many know little about the content of world religions, and are, even in countries formed through Christian influences, often estranged from their own heritage and culture. European literature, art, and music are saturated with Christian, and specifically Biblical, allusions, which now may be little understood. When any culture has been formed over the centuries by a specific faith, indifference to it produces significant change. Education is bound to remain a central issue for ideas of faith, when different views of society, and different 'worldviews', clash. It remains central for the transmission of culture. Parental views of what is morally important, perhaps stemming from different religions, can be at odds with what may be taught in the State schools of different countries. Some see dangers in the control of ideas and beliefs by any State, and suggest that it strikes at the roots of democracy. The latter certainly thrives on freedom to hold different understandings of what is basically important in human life.

Faith as an ethical guide

The excessive stress on science as the arbiter of truth resulted after the Second World War in some philosophers seeing moral judgements as expressions of emotion, or personal attitudes, not claims to truth. Morality was turned into a personal intention to live a particular way of life. A Cambridge philosopher, R. B. Braithwaite, made religion simply a matter of moral policy and action. In trying to protect Christianity, in particular, from the depredations of a scientistic view, he claimed that the 'primary use of religious assertions' was to 'announce allegiance to a set of moral principles'. They in turn involved the mere intention to live a particular kind of life, in the Christian case 'an agapeistic way of life'. To the retort that you do not need to be a Christian to show love to others, his reply was that what made it Christian, rather than, say, Jewish, or Buddhist, was that similar actions could be associated with 'thinking of different *stories*'.

This is similar to Wittgenstein's view that Christians entertain certain 'pictures' to guide their life inspiration. For a Christian, therefore, the New Testament becomes simply literature, like Shakespeare's plays, or Greek tragedy. They can move and inspire us, and religious writings may do the same. The stories Jesus told in parable form to guide us perform the same function as the 'stories' of Jesus's life, miracles, and death. The intention to live a particular kind of life becomes important, with the weight put on moral behaviour. 'Works' define the faith. There is, though, a distinction between the moral influence of fictional narratives in literature, potent though that may be, and claims to alleged eternal truths as guides for humanity. Pointing to universal truths about the human condition in fiction seems different from the specific claims of revealed religion.

Removing the connection between faith and perceived truth puts more focus on the role of the imagination. We should never discount the part imagination can play in the pursuit of truth itself. Simply following the model of scientific investigation in religion and looking for 'theories' and 'evidence' ignores the nexus between religious faith, the human heart, and moral action. Even science has its visionaries, eager to explore the limits of human knowledge. All reasoning depends on imagination, and the use of allegory and analogy, to reach out to the limits of human comprehension. Faith uses reason, but that should not be confined within a cold and impersonal 'rationalism'. It needs all the resources of human understanding. Christianity and other religions may not be only sets of stories, but stories can be means of illumination and motives for action. Faith steers emotions, as well as satisfying the intellect. So far from being an arid conclusion of a deductive argument, it can be a spur to a greater appreciation of the relations between truth, beauty, and goodness. The stories of faith may try to be more than that but they do inspire action. Imagination helps faith to reach towards what appears almost beyond human comprehension.

Someone who tried to harness the strengths of both reason and imagination was C. S. Lewis, the 20th-century scholar of literature at both Oxford and Cambridge. He became a Christian apologist, and a writer of children's literature. His *Narnia Chronicles*, exploiting allegory and myth, have become widely known, not least through television and film. Lewis was particularly anxious, while upholding the truth of Christianity, not to imprison it in an austere rationalism. He used myth, and visual images, to illustrate what he believed to be true. For Lewis, Christian faith is reasonable and enables us to see what is real, even if it cannot always be expressed concisely in language. One dictum not only expresses his views, but itself powerfully uses imagery. He said: 'I believe in Christianity as I believe the sun has risen, not only because I see it, but because by it I see everything else.' For Lewis, a Christian vision could bring things into sharp focus, and the imagination could roam beyond what seemed possible within a narrowly scientific approach.

Through stories and myths it can illuminate what might be possible, and that itself could be a sign of truth.

Talk of stories can echo the work of 20th-century theologians such as Rudolf Bultmann, who wanted to 'de-mythologize' Christianity by reinterpreting and regarding its references to the supernatural in terms of 'myth'. That might be a theological term of art, but its use changes the subject from what myths purport to be about to their meaning for participants in a religion, particularly as shown in moral action. A distinction has been drawn by some Christian theologians between the so-called 'Jesus of history' and the 'Christ of faith'. They were following existentialist philosophy in concentrating on the meaning a belief has for people's lives. They were also responding to the Biblical criticism and historical research which had arisen in the 19th century. Often itself driven by unargued philosophical positions, it tended to look at historical records through the assumptions of modern science which tended to cast suspicion on references to the supernatural.

If miracles cannot happen, historical records describing them must be false, or interpreted differently, so as to be seen as 'just stories'. The records may express the prior faith of the writers, and that private faith would lead to the accretion of legend and myth about Jesus. Accordingly, historical records, including reports from alleged eye-witnesses, had, it seemed, to be reinterpreted. Once it was consciously accepted that the Christ of faith is a figment of literary imagination, a believer could not remain wholeheartedly committed to such a figure. Why risk one's life, or make personal sacrifices, merely for a story, however inspiring? Theologians contrasted what they regarded as 'living witness and faith' with something rejected as 'improbable scientific fact'. That remark was published in 1977 when some Christian theology was still retreating before a simple-minded empiricist view of science. Nevertheless, the contrast has seeped into wider culture, and remains there.

Severing links between faith and claims to objective truth ensures that the character of religious faith will change as society changes. Faith, it will seem, must be 'relevant' to the contemporary age, and reflect its assumptions. Another theologian of the 1970s insisted that the 'preached Christ is not the historical Jesus'. As times change, and societies alter, the argument was that the 'preached Christ must surely be a changing figure'. That is reasonable, if, say, Christianity should just meet the perceived needs of humans in the 21st century, rather than recount possible events of 2,000 years ago. The conditions of contemporary society, it is said, are vastly different from the cultural context of the Roman Empire, in which Christianity was first preached. Just as a faith that does not speak to contemporary needs is useless, no worthwhile faith can be a simple reflection of contemporary needs if it has anything important to say. This is a tension that other faiths may face, as evidenced in the stresses between 'liberal' and more traditional forms of Judaism. Islam, in many countries, is more resistant to contemporary pressures, often dismissed as 'Western', but it may be difficult always to ignore them.

Any faith that merely reflects contemporary fashions, and the attitudes of the people who hold it, will change as societies change. The same applies to different geographical contexts. Christian faith in Africa, say, may then have to be very different from that in the United States. It would seem then that any faith is just about 'us', differing according to who 'we' may be. The substance of faith changes and carries different moral assumptions when it reflects different social circumstances. Society then determines faith, rather than faith providing a prophetic voice for society. We could wonder whether contemporary Christians hold the same faith as the members of the early Church. The distinction between the Christ of faith and the Jesus of history makes explicit the theological conclusion that 'Christ changes as societies change'. Those words were written fifty years ago, and that means that the Christ of that faith fifty years ago could be irrelevant to the present world. The 'Christ of faith' seems no longer an anchor, or an unchanging guide, but a constantly changing and flickering image, projected by our own temporary situations.

Morality without faith?

Morality can be costly, involving a genuine concern for others for their own sake. It is different from prudence and certainly cannot be an instrument for one's own selfish purposes. The question 'why be moral?' is a definite challenge that needs an answer. We must believe other people matter, so that their interests seem as important as our own. Some may think that correct action is more important than correct doctrine, but that assumes that we know how to assess 'correct' action. We have to rely on teaching and experience, or, in other words, 'doctrine'. We have to know what we believe, and why that should affect the way we live.

Modern proponents of liberalism and political philosophy have made human autonomy the central issue. Yet when we each do as we wish, we, literally, or metaphorically, collide with each other. Freedom must be constrained, by law and morality, so that we respect each other's interests. The 19th-century political philosopher J. S. Mill invoked the principle that we should not harm others. Why, though, should I worry about harming others if that does not harm myself? Just as significant is what counts as 'harm'. We cannot avoid fundamental questions about humans, their needs, and why they are important.

Appeals to avoiding harm often do not settle moral arguments. There are profound disagreements in any pluralist society about the purpose of society, the nature of family units, the right moral teaching for children, and the relevance of religious belief itself. Is the breakdown of marriage as an institution going to be harmful? Different moral responses to assisted suicide and euthanasia draw on different beliefs about the possible 'sanctity' of human life weighed against the avoidance of suffering. They involve different judgements of what is harmful. Seeing the image of God in fellow humans can be a powerful guide to action, not least because seen as a truth valid across generations. When faith reflects a particular society's obsessions, it does not, as it perhaps should, challenge the moral standards of the day, and witness to something better. Faith must look beyond fashionable assumptions, if it is more than a personal or social programme of moral and political action.

Following Nietzsche, many philosophers have seen morality as a cynical exercise of power over others. The question he boldly faced is whether everything can stay the same when there is no longer faith in a truth which traditionally sustained beliefs about the worth of human beings. This is not a new question. In the 19th century, Matthew Arnold stood on Dover beach in England, watching the tide go out and hearing the ebbing water sucking back the pebbles. To his mind, in his famous poem, it illustrated the way 'the sea of faith' was once 'at the full' and now retreats with a 'melancholy, long withdrawing roar'. He recognized that without such faith, the world would be seen differently. It 'hath really neither joy, nor love, nor light, nor certitude, nor peace, nor help for pain'.

A world without faith to illuminate it might not seem the same, or provide any inspiration for meaningful human activity. Love could be an illusion. A godless world seemed a pitiless world in which ultimately nothing, not even the most important of human concerns, carried meaning or purpose. According to some evolutionary biologists, the whole of human life has developed through blind, and chance, processes. We might, through our nature, be encouraged to look after our families and spread our genes. We might indulge in what is confusingly called 'reciprocal' altruism, helping others so as to get something back for ourselves. The problem is then that pure altruism, in the form of genuine concern for others for their own sake, seems impossible, too costly for individuals, and winnowed out through evolution.

From a scientific point of view, 'facts' are totally different from 'values', with the former referring to what can be established by science. The implicit understanding seems to be that 'our' values, or moral standards, are not 'facts' or part of the scheme of things, but express attitudes to whatever happens. Paradoxically, appeals to human rights are as common as reference to values even though such 'rights' imply that there is something special about being human. That reintroduces the idea that morality appeals to characteristics inherent in reality, which suggests that rights are more than 'values' that happen to be held. Locke, with ideas that profoundly influenced the founding of the United States, had maintained that we are all equal, and ought not to harm the 'life, liberty, health or possessions' of others. These are the basic ideas of a liberal philosophy, but his reason for respecting them is often forgotten. He believed that the reason was because 'we are all the workmanship of one omnipotent and infinitely wise Maker', and servants of 'one sovereign Master'. Many would in the present age reject that theological underpinning, arising from Locke's own faith. The foundations of any humanism are fragile without it, and often rely on apparently arbitrary personal decisions to respect others.

What counts as human flourishing is itself a basic moral issue. Sincere moral disagreements come from disputes about what is important for human beings, and what they need. The nature of such flourishing can be morally contested, and moral decisions are rooted in wider questions about our view of the world. Even an atheist morality, such as forms of humanism, evinces a faith that needs rational support. It posits the centrality of humanity, often trusting the essential goodness of human nature and the reliability of science in ways that go beyond the available evidence but need rational grounds. If, though, morality is like religion in needing some rational basis, and if it may even often be intimately linked with religious views, it must be prepared with religion to join in public debate and examination. That in turn raises the issue of the possible relation between faith, conscience, and public law, to which we now turn.

Chapter 6
Faith and law

Public faith

Faith could be left alone, if considered a private matter, but religious beliefs are manifested in public. Religious beliefs often have implications for wider society, and will come within the ambit of public law. Article 9 of the European Convention of Human Rights (sponsored by the Council of Europe, not the European Union) recognizes an absolute right to 'freedom of thought, conscience and religion'. Private thoughts are sacrosanct and cannot be outlawed. Once they are demonstrated in public, the Convention recognizes that their application can be limited in the interests of 'public safety, for the protection of public order, health or morals, or for the protection of the rights and freedoms of others'. Not everything is permissible when it is manifested in the name of some religion. Human sacrifice sometimes has had a religious motivation but cannot be tolerated in a free and democratic society. Reference, though, to 'the protection of morals' hardly settles matters, when the content of morality is often contested. One recurring issue is what happens when 'freedom of thought, conscience and religion' clashes with other rights, such as that to equality. Can one right trump another, or should rights be kept in balance, and a compromise reached? Many hold that there is no 'hierarchy' of rights, and some advocate what is termed 'reasonable accommodation' between rights.

In the case of freedom of religion, much depends on how religious faith is to be defined, and how far it is seen as conducive to a good society. Like the United Nations Universal Declaration of Human Rights (Article 18), the European Convention couples it with thought and conscience. The phrase 'religion or belief' is used and broadly construed, with reference to freedom of religion. This contrasts with the First Amendment of the Constitution of the United States, which states baldly that 'Congress shall make no law respecting an establishment of religion, or protecting the free exercise thereof'. Dealing with religion alone, it ignores the vaguer concepts of conscience and belief. Associating religion with belief puts the emphasis on individual judgement. Once faith involves a more collective aspect, the Universal Declaration of Human Rights and the European Convention give it only qualified protection. The manifestation of 'religion or belief' is explicitly distinguished from the core part of religion, understood as individual and private. The further practice of religion 'alone or in community' and 'in public or in private' becomes a qualified right.

This distinction is linked to a theological distinction made in the Middle Ages between a *forum internum*, the private sphere comprising a person's interior life, and a *forum externum*, the public aspect consisting of an individual's observable actions and behaviour. The distinction was originally built into the Roman Catholic Church's canon law, and has influenced the division between belief and practice in secular law. The public exercise of faith can seem threatening, and the role of the internal forum becomes very circumscribed. Even a totalitarian government might allow people to believe what they wish if it is never manifested in word or action.

Much depends on how far faith is private. If faith and works cannot be separated, manifesting faith will be crucial to its integrity. The United States Constitution is forthright in its protection of religious practice. One Justice of the American Supreme Court in an Opinion for the Court has said: 'The

Constitution protects not just the right to be a religious person holding beliefs inwardly and secretly; it also protects the right to *act* on those beliefs outwardly and publicly.' He sums up the situation by saying: 'The right to be religious without the right to *do* religious things would hardly amount to a right at all.' He was particularly concerned about the ability of the government 'to intrude so much in matters of faith'.

Freedom for religion?

Public law is involved when faith emerges from behind the closed doors of churches, mosques, synagogues, and other religious buildings. Judgements about the potential harm of religious activities to society must be made. The clash of freedom of religion with other rights comes to the fore. What is to count as religion? Should faith of a non-religious kind be given legal protection? The stress on freedom of religion *or belief* in charters of human rights raises the issue of what other beliefs will be respected. They could be grounded in deep issues of conscience, and disparate ones will jostle for attention, even when unconnected with religion. Philosophical beliefs, such as vegetarianism or pacifism, claim protection from the law in various jurisdictions. When accommodation, though, is offered beyond religious belief in 'the transcendent' (or its denial), the law can lose focus and religious faith its central importance.

The phrase 'religion or belief' can attenuate any claim to religious freedom to breaking point. Not every sincere belief is a reason for a principled refusal to observe the law. Conscientious objection to killing people in time of war is different from an alleged conscientious objection to paying taxes. Coupling 'religion' with the idea of 'belief' privatizes faith, and suggests that religious faith itself is of no social significance. The reference to religion as the first freedom in the American First Amendment is thought by many to be intentional. James Madison, a major influence and later American President, accepted, like other Founders, the centrality of religious influence on public life, and the importance of religious freedom as a foundation for a free society. A forced faith, they thought, could not be genuine, nor contribute to genuine democracy.

The First Amendment assumed that religious faith is special. Scholars sometimes point out that it echoed the First Clause of the English Magna Carta, sealed at Runnymede, near Windsor, by King John in 1215. Still theoretically in force, it guaranteed the freedom of the 'English church' (*ecclesia Anglicana*). Following a vicious dispute with the Pope and the Church in England, King John closed all churches for worship for a considerable time. The subsequent undertaking was given to an institution, not individuals, and underlines how religious faith has both a communal and individual dimension. The tension between social and private aspects of faith, between public manifestation and personal belief, remains a reality. Increasing secularization has often pushed religion to the margins of society. Freedom of religion is sometimes reduced to the possibility of freedom of worship. That is an important element, but only an element, of the manifestation of religious faith. Arguments rage about what protection law should offer to other forms religious expression.

Some philosophers of law, even in the United States, are sceptical of the idea that religious faith should be given any special protection at all by law. They do not see religion as warranting any more special treatment than does a general liberty of conscience. So far from religious faith being special in any way, they sometimes see it as particularly threatening, perhaps because of a feared dogmatism and intolerance. Some see all religious faith as irrational, harmful, and even false, and think it sensible to control it. For them it is an inappropriate part of public life, perhaps not to be tolerated even in a free society. That, though, is to assume they themselves have a full grasp on what can be true, and that is often what is in question. Unless, too, all views can be exposed to public view, they may fester beneath the surface of social life, perhaps breaking out in radical and extreme ways. Concentrating on the subjective element in faith can focus on some believers' dogmatism and resistance to criticism. The possible importance of what is ignored changes into the political problem of dealing with awkward people and groups.

The role of conscience

When people of faith contribute to democratic argument, they view the common good in ways that can clash with secular outlooks. Different religions may themselves differ, but in pluralist societies we still live together, and it is sensible to work towards a convergence of views, or at least some compromise and accommodation. The modern quest for human rights began with the realization that minorities can be at risk even in a democracy. After genocide in the Second World War, the United Nations proclaimed a system of basic human rights that could protect any group or individual at odds with the prevailing view of their society. The example of the Jews showed that while race may be a recurrent factor in ill-treatment, religious faith is not far behind. In the case of Jews, the two were closely linked. Respect for human rights, such as the right to religious liberty, can protect those on the losing side of a democratic argument and be enshrined in law.

The influence of religious faith on attitudes and behaviour may upset social cohesion by keeping people apart from the mainstream of society. Jews and Christians have often faced persecution, and are still doing so in many countries, as do adherents of other religions. Muslims in the current age set themselves apart in many nations by choosing distinctive dress. The full-face veil for women is controversial, and the wearing of the headscarf by women has been in the recent past the subject of legal action, even in countries with Islamic roots such as Turkey. Wearing a cross became an issue in some work contexts in the United Kingdom. Arguments about such differences in dress and jewellery stand proxy for deeper controversies about the rights of individuals to manifest their religious commitment in public.

Any democratic society must make collective decisions about what is and is not legal. What, though, should happen if religious faith encourages people to resist what the State demands? The classic example has been conscientious objection in a time of war. Seeing religious faith as a species of conscience avoids tricky decisions, which courts prefer to avoid, about what constitutes genuine religion, so that they do not have to treat it as special. Some contend that singling out religion gives it a misplaced priority in a democratic state. When, though, religious freedom is subordinated to some ideal of equal treatment and equality, even in an apparent moral vacuum, we still have to ask why the law ought to treat people equally. Most societies throughout history have not championed equality, nor respected conscience, and it is often inconvenient for the powerful to do so. The implicit answer may be that this is what 'we' happen to agree about now, whoever 'we' happen to be, but that is an insubstantial basis for a moral, or legal, policy. Who agrees and on what grounds? That already seems to presuppose that we are free and equal citizens, who should severally act in accord with what we believe is most important in life.

None of this explains why respect should be given to whatever anyone thinks important. People's lives may revolve around loyalty to Manchester United Football Club, so they never miss a game. If an employer demands that they work instead of attending an important match, is that improper, and to be prohibited in law? Is it different when someone wants attend public worship in accordance with their religious obligations? Attending a football game might appear to some as sacrosanct as the observance of a Sabbath. Once the law has to protect personal preferences and hobbies, however important to individuals, no law can claim general applicability. Everyone will ask for exemptions, the law gains no purchase, and everyone becomes their own law-giver.

No State could countenance such a situation. Lines must be drawn, perhaps so that the law should not allow any exceptions, or accommodations. It should treat everyone in the same way, 'without fear or favour'. Faith, conscience, and individual loyalties seem too subjective. Perhaps religious faith, and even conscience in general, should not expect any privileges. Everyone should then acquiesce in what the law enjoins, once a social policy is enshrined in law. This raises dilemmas, especially in medicine. Should doctors and nurses be compelled, if they are to remain in their profession, to undertake procedures, such as abortion or euthanasia, which are against their conscience? Many medical practitioners believe in the autonomy of the patient, and this too raises a question. Why, say, should the autonomy of a personal decision to receive euthanasia override the autonomy of medical staff who believed they entered the medical profession to save life, not end it? The moral integrity of medical staff is as much at stake as that of the patients.

Some political philosophers hold that individual exemptions can be defended because their moral force lies in their importance to individual integrity, not in the advancement of a supposed objective or collective good such as religion. Conscience must then be respected because of its role in a personal feeling of identity, and people must be true to themselves. The idea of being answerable to any objective truth recedes, as does the idea that faith is important because of what it claims. Why, though, do personal autonomy and integrity matter? Like 'equality', and even 'justice', they are key notions in some political philosophy, but there must still be a reason for faith in their importance. The perennial danger is that many may be living unthinkingly off the capital of what has been bequeathed by the Christian faith of previous generations, while rejecting the faith that underpins their assumptions.

Faith and democracy

Some resist claims to objective truth, on the grounds that they disparage those who hold different views. When fellow citizens are by implication judged to be mistaken, or even morally wicked, that allegedly undermines their dignity. Claims to truth in ethical matters seem divisive and anti-democratic, setting one group of citizens above another. Yet the need for democracy itself arises because people often disagree. Notions of dignity, personal autonomy, and our obligation to respect them are themselves deeply ethical. Whether 'values' should be imposed by one person, one group, or even the State is itself a deeply moral issue. Resisting any claim to objective truth in morality just relies on a different set of moral truths. We are driven back to questions about human nature, and which principles should guide our action. We cannot criticize the idea of moral truth, and at the same time take a moral stand on the importance of human dignity, or autonomy.

Democracy needs a joint endeavour in pursuit of whatever is the common good, particularly when there are divergent conceptions of what that is. Modern law in a pluralist State tries to be like an impartial referee in a game, administering the rules when different teams confront each other. However, the nature of the rules can be disputed, and often rest on implicit moral assumptions. States often aim to keep faith communities, and matters of faith, at arm's length, and courts in many jurisdictions take pride in a supposed moral neutrality. They should still treat everyone impartially, but even impartiality, as a requirement of justice, cannot exist in a moral vacuum. Ideas of justice, fairness, and equality must be built into the basic assumptions of any law that does not just serve the immediate interests of the State. Law courts themselves should be guided by some faith in what is just and right, if they are not to be the mere servants of power.

Even if law is guided by basic moral principles, there are still clashes of moral outlook. The law may have to take sides, but many would hold that it could respect fundamental moral differences, by providing reasonable accommodations in certain cases. The point of democracy is that alternative views and the freedom to live by them must be fostered. Minority views can sometimes become those of the majority later. Sometimes laws without exemptions bear down heavily on those obliged by their religious faith to dissent from what is legally required. Some accommodations can be made at trivial cost, as when Sikh police or service personnel are allowed to wear turbans rather than helmets. Other exemptions may be controversial, but still morally appropriate, as for pacifists exempted from military service, though not perhaps from other forms of national service.

Religious faith is an obvious target for the legal system of a society recognizing no authority beyond itself. When seen as simply a property of individuals, defining their identity, the question is how far those individuals can be tolerated. If it claims, though, to concern a transcendent reality, against which societies and governments can be judged, it will appear more threatening. Such faith calls into question the ultimate authority and legitimacy of a ruthless regime and will always be persecuted by an unscrupulous State.

Civil and religious law

For religious believers a crucial issue can often be whether the law of the land coerces them into doing what they believe is morally wrong. One way out of this impasse is to make civil and religious obligations coincide. Islam's stress on submission or obedience echoes the way in which Muslim faith is built on the idea of a law that lays down detailed instructions for behaviour. This is particularly important in areas of family law and the treatment of women. The goal of Muslims in some countries is to close the gap between civil and religious law, so the State becomes aligned with the demands of the Qu'ran, as mediated in *sharia* law. Some call this 'theocracy', as if God is immediately involved, but relevant texts can be understood differently in different schools of thought. That can cause difficulties for any proclamation of a single *sharia* law. In the majority Sunni branch of Islam, there is no clerical hierarchy, no equivalent of bishops or Pope, to give authoritative rulings, but a reliance on networks of scholars, providing varying interpretations.

A further problem, appreciated in universities in some Islamic countries, is how *sharia* and divine revelation in general interact with wider areas of human knowledge, such as contemporary philosophy and science. A debate about the role of human reason, and its interaction with tradition, raged in the early, formative years of Islam. In some ways, it was similar to modern Christian questioning about the interaction of faith and reason. There was controversy about the authority of Hadiths, sayings and reported acts attributed to the Prophet Muhammad, but in more recent centuries there has often been a tendency to take a more restricted, literal approach to all the instructions perceived in such texts.

Although obedience to religious law is of paramount importance to Islam, indeed its essence, some think there has to be at root a role for something like faith. The Qu'ran is the foundation of Islam, and its words claim to be a direct revelation from God. There lies its power. A contemporary Muslim writer, Mustafa Akyol, asks the question whether the Prophet created the Qu'ran or the Qu'ran the Prophet. He claims that believing the latter is what makes a Muslim. Intriguingly, he accepts that that is 'an article of faith, which requires a leap of faith', but maintains it is a credible leap. For a Muslim, the Qur'an contains God's words to Muhammad, and all else, including obedience, follows from that. It is God's law, not the person of Muhammad, who is the focus. Interestingly, the same dynamic occurs at least in the stricter forms of Orthodox Judaism. A foundation of its belief is the divine authorship of the five books of Moses in the Bible, the Pentateuch. That faith supports the entire framework of Jewish law and validates the idea of a way of life depending entirely on obedience to the laws laid down in the books. It is at the heart of much Orthodox understanding of what the Jewish religion is about.

This obedience to law both in Islam and in Judaism is markedly different from its place in a Christian view of faith. Shabbir Akhtar, a Muslim theologian, comments on what he terms the 'Muslim predilection for jurisprudence and a corresponding aversion to theology'. In his Letter to the Galatians, one of the earliest New Testament writings, St Paul distinguishes Christianity from traditional legalistic views precisely by invoking the concept of faith. He declares that 'we have put our faith in Jesus Christ, in order that we may be justified through this faith, and not through actions dictated by law'. Inward trust should motivate us, not the demands of an external law, in this case Jewish religious law. This notion of justification, as we have seen, carries with it the idea of being made right with God, of being vindicated, as in a court of law. Our innermost attitudes, beliefs, and motives matter more than our conformity with a set of rules. Trust, or faith, comes first, and obedience to a way of life after. Even in Judaism there is often a recognition that mere 'legalism', following the letter of the law, is insufficient. People should not just do what is right but be virtuous in having the right intentions. Action should be accompanied by an understanding of why it is important to obey laws.

Some think that rules, or 'laws', do not matter at all, only having the right motives, such as love. St Paul, in the early Church, had to battle with those who held that faith gave them licence to do what they liked. Rules and laws may be helpful, even necessary as guides, but their deeper purpose was held to be a matter of manifesting love of God and love of neighbour. Following the letter of the law may not be an end in itself, but an undefined 'love' motivating people in an unfocused way could become self-indulgent. Christ came, as He said, to 'fulfil' the law, not abolish it.

The different approaches to 'law' show how different Muslim and Christian views of faith can be. As Shabbir Akhtar comments: 'Only the New Testament sharply distinguishes faith in divine promises from faithfulness to the Law.' He himself sees the latter as 'the right means for being right with God', exemplifying the obedience that characterizes Islam. Yet the centrality for Muslims of law, as expressed in *sharia* law, can produce tension with some civil laws. Many countries, with varying religious and legal heritages of their own, have struggled to accommodate it, particularly in economic and family matters. That encourages some to keep all religion firmly on the private side of the divide between public and private, and to insulate public law from suspicion of religious bias, or any religious influence, but there lies a paradox. As an example, England is in origin a deeply Christian society, with the origins of its legal system stretching back far beyond Magna Carta to Alfred, the Anglo-Saxon King of Wessex in the 9th century. Christianity profoundly influenced his view of law, and its subsequent development. Once the faith has faded away that gave life to the basic principles of justice and fairness, equality before the law and individual freedom, the haunting question is how long a commitment to them will continue.

The adherence of faith to perceived truth, and the wish to stamp out error, is expressed most forcibly in laws of blasphemy. In a democracy, such laws appear to infringe important rights to free speech, and freedom of religion, rights which, many would hold, are themselves buttressed by religious belief. Freedom of belief is circumscribed when one cannot even make calm and rational criticism of any religious belief. Blasphemy laws protect dominant religions and can bear down heavily on minority religions. Even in England and Wales, a blasphemy law remained on the books, though rarely enforced, until 2008. There is, though, a particular problem for minorities in countries imposing *sharia* law on everyone. The feeling that some citizens are not treated equally comes to the fore when blasphemy laws in Muslim countries enforce adherence by everyone to *sharia* law. They can be used to prevent alleged heresy and stop the promulgation of other faiths.

A blasphemy law can prevent offensive and inflammatory attacks on a religion, stirring up hatred and violence, as do laws against the incitement of religious hatred. The latter, however, fall short of the more wide-ranging laws, advocated by some, that prohibit words and actions that are merely perceived by people of one faith or another as offensive. That inhibits the freedom openly to discuss and criticize the religious beliefs of different faiths. The focus would not then be proposed truth, but the shifting sensibilities of believers. Guarding and teaching its claims to truth is important for any religion but can be destructive of the search for truth. The mediaeval Inquisition of the Roman Catholic Church, lasting in some places until the Napoleonic Wars in the early 19th century, enforced orthodoxy by law. Its aim was to stamp out heresy, but such laws can outlaw all forms of dissent. The core of human freedom contains the ability to examine all faith and even adopt a new one. The use of law to impose some orthodoxy, and coerce those who dissent, prevents that.

Mediaeval jurists in Islam considered that blasphemy was a capital crime. The same view can be found in some modern Islamic jurisdictions, so that adherents of other faiths risk serious persecution. The Qu'ran itself is fairly silent about blasphemy and blasphemers, merely warning against association with them. Islam has often appeared more protective of the Prophet even than of God, perhaps on the principle that God can look after Himself. That is an important insight, in that however much the alleged truth of some faith is upheld, its ultimate defence would appropriately be left by a believer to the Judge of all. 'Blasphemy' can easily become an instrument of human power, and there are parallel instances of 'secular' blasphemy, so that criticism of a regime is tantamount to treason. Religious faith and national loyalties can all be harnessed for political ends. All faith is thereby corrupted, becoming an instrument for other interests, in a struggle for power.

Chapter 7
Faith and society

The goal of truth

The modern Western world has become increasingly secular, trying to function without regard to religious influences. We should, it seems, have a 'naked public square'. At times, this has been taken literally when the presence of a commemorative cross or tablets containing the Ten Commandments in public places has been contested. Some have objected to the display of Christmas trees in city squares, which are then only allowed to survive as 'holiday trees'. When such symbols are tolerated, they are often regarded as legacies of the past rather than proclamations of truth to the present. Even in democratic countries, politicians with a noticeable religious faith can be viewed with suspicion, and even driven from office. Why should that be? In a free society, people should make their own minds up about faith, and be free to practise it. Legislators are often warned, even by political theorists, not to bring their faith into the legislative chamber. Laws, it seems, should not be passed because of religious principle. The continuing assumption is that faith, as the antithesis of reason, makes no useful contribution to public debate.

Faith in God demands recognition of an authority beyond the reach of the State, and even in a democracy that can be uncomfortable. The voice of a conscience driven by religious faith can challenge activities that people do not want challenged. At the end of the 18th century, those making a good living from the slave trade did not welcome evangelical Christians campaigning for its abolition. Religious faith points to an objective standard of what is good and bad, right and wrong, and makes people accountable to something beyond their own desires and interests. It can seem absolutist, refusing to acknowledge contrary positions. Even those advocating religious freedom are often accused of seeking religious privilege, so that such freedom appears the enemy of equality. When people are free to hold different beliefs, there will be different beliefs on offer, but divergences of opinion about what is true still matter. When we care about what is true, it is self-defeating, even if more comfortable, to shut ourselves within our own prejudices and leave them unchallenged. Diversity of belief, even about religion, is a challenge, not a desirable conclusion.

People cannot be mistaken, or judged adversely by others, if there are no objective standards to anchor what is true. Without truth as a goal, everything becomes ultimately pointless and purposeless. We could not hope to agree in principle on any common course of action with our fellow citizens. There is nothing to agree about, and we are threatened with the total fragmentation of any society. People who believe in nothing are liable to believe anything.

Any claim about matters that transcend human knowledge must concede that such knowledge must be incomplete. Monotheism must recognize the importance of humility before a God who surpasses human understanding and is not a human construction. That may be important, but the fact of competing worldviews should not make us forget the importance of truth as a goal. A faith that is not dogmatic may still be confident in its own judgement, even amid great diversity of belief. Everyone, whether religious or not, ultimately needs some form of faith to give a direction to life. We are all human, sharing the same human nature, and face a reality that outstrips our full understanding, whether in science or beyond. We have to go on living and acting, even when matters may be less than demonstrably certain, and the truth of many beliefs, even beyond religion, can be rationally doubted.

Dogmatism, certainty, and coercion

When people 'of faith' claim absolute certainty, an intolerant dogmatism could threaten social cohesion. The post-modernist Italian philosopher, Gianni Vattimo, baldly maintained that 'wherever politics purports to seek truth, there cannot be democracy'. An authoritarian and coercive religion could be dangerous, but many allege that claiming objective truth threatens others' freedom. Vattimo asserts: 'It paves the way to the republic of the philosophers, the experts, the technicians, and, at the limit, the ethical state.' Some can think they know what is good for others, regardless of what those citizens may themselves prefer.

Democracies are founded on the idea of individual freedom, but that can be challenged by the rise of a bureaucracy that becomes unaccountable because of its claims to expert knowledge. 'Experts', like anyone with sincere, and well-intentioned, beliefs, can be proved wrong, particularly when confronting new situations. Economic crises are rarely predicted by economic forecasters. The spread of a new virus, or its variant, may challenge existing medical knowledge. This should not undermine a provisional respect for expert opinion but removes any idea of infallibility. Confident assurance cannot guarantee truth. Trusting expert knowledge can itself involve a new leap of faith. As with arguments about the role of religious authorities and their influence on faith, all claims to secular authority have to be justified, unless they wish to rely simply on brute power.

Understanding the tentative nature of even the best claims to knowledge should not involve rejecting the possibility of truth, or our human ability to track it. Some know more than others, but the existence of objective truth does not guarantee anyone's ability to grasp it fully. We should not lapse into scepticism and think we cannot know anything at all. That would be absurd, and result in paralysis. The quest for knowledge has a point, even if certainty is a psychological category, and does not guarantee accuracy. The possession of knowledge must not mean that anyone should feel able to impose their beliefs on others, without their full consent and cooperation. Paternalist coercion in the interests of those being coerced is alien to any idea of the consent and freedom of citizens in a democracy. They should, within reason, be able to live according to their own judgements about where truth lies.

How is this relevant to religious faith in society? Democratic politics assumes disagreement rather than agreement as its basis. There would be no need for democratic votes if we all instinctively agreed about everything. Democracy needs an agreed framework in which people can argue for different views to operate, but there needs to be space for such diversity. When religious faith is forbidden from full expression in the body politic, many ordinary citizens cannot advocate, or act on, what they believe most important in life, and might be important for a society. Silencing views that happen to be unpopular, whether religious, political, or whatever, is the antithesis of democratic freedom and discussion. It can destroy it. The usual rejoinder, we have seen, is that faith is different because of its irrationality, and dogmatic certainty. It can though be advantageous for those dismissing religious faith to recognize that if it is claiming truth, it can then be publicly questioned and challenged. Apparent certainty, however comforting psychologically, cannot guarantee infallibility, and the world has always been full of people who have been certain and wrong about many things.

Religious faith invites suspicion because of the fanaticism that sometimes seems to accompany it, encouraging the intolerant compulsion of others. That, though, raises the issue as to whether coercion can be consistent with any idea of human freedom, particularly religiously inspired ones. A traditional answer, even in a religious context, was that 'error has no rights'. Totalitarian governments have not hesitated to coerce their citizens into acting in accordance with what is regarded by the State as good for them (or at least good for the State). That is also a temptation for a dominant religion in many parts of the world. In Christianity, ideas of individual freedom, and responsibility, have loomed large in recent centuries. As John Locke, and his American followers in the 18th century, trenchantly argued, compelled faith, requiring outward conformity rather than inward devotion, cannot be genuine.

The crucial idea of human dignity is now often linked with the importance of personal autonomy. Some notions of autonomy are at odds with traditional views of faith, suggesting to the contemporary mind the absolute right of individuals not just to choose freely, but to decide for themselves what is to count as good or bad, or even true or false. Any commitment to external standards, whether imposed by the State or purely metaphysical, seems to compromise individuals' sense of their own identity. Subjectivist views of faith as personal construction, rather than discovery, fit comfortably with this. The paradox is that the concept of human dignity only gains traction because it appears to refer to a basic truth about the value of human beings, and their nature, that does not depend on assumptions that just happen to be generally held in a particular society at a particular time.

In pluralist societies, there are disagreements about the very idea of human nature, particularly if a supernatural and transcendent realm is invoked. Many visions of faith share that basic vision of a divine realm beyond this world, with a contrast drawn with 'naturalist' presuppositions that restrict all vision to a world accessible by science. They may also agree about the inherent dignity of humans. When all religious faith can be seen as similar, the contrast between it and 'naturalist' views is often the basic issue. Despite such commonalities, differences in belief and moral priorities between different religious outlooks must be confronted honestly. Discounting them results in all religious belief being belittled because none of its content is then being taken seriously.

Religious faith does not always speak with one voice about human freedom. It is still a major issue for some religions, such as Islam, when faced with those born into the faith wishing to commit themselves to a different one. They are still accused in some countries of 'apostasy' and can be severely punished. Individual freedom, and our final accountability before God, may be considered central beliefs for Christianity, but Christians themselves have not always respected it. Cynics have said that when the Church feels weak, it talks of freedom, and when it feels strong it talks about truth. The Roman Catholic Inquisition was an example of this, but other Christian denominations have sometimes used their power, not least when they have functioned as an established State Church. State recognition may give acknowledgement of the role religion plays in public life, but it should never grow into a coercive support for a religious outlook, let alone interference in the promulgation of doctrines. At times, as in 17th-century Stuart England, before the Glorious Revolution and the 1689 Act of Toleration, national governments have been too ready to suppress alternative beliefs, even avowedly Christian ones.

There is a jump from thinking one has knowledge to coercing others. Presupposing that there is such a thing as truth, assuming we possess it in entirety, and then thinking we can impose it on others are three different steps. One does not need to give up on the idea of truth to realize the fact of human fallibility and finitude in all areas of purported knowledge. Truth may not always be within our grasp, but even if we think we have knowledge, our supposed understanding of God may teach us that just as we relish our own freedom, we ought to respect the God-given freedom of others. Coercion and a failure to respect the intrinsic dignity of our fellow human beings undermines democracy. It is the pursuit of power, not truth, and challenges the basis of all religion, not just Christianity.

Conviction and doubt

Any society needs enough shared understandings to be able to function without being paralysed by dissension. Human beings want stability and a certainty that is grounded in more than transient agreements. Nietzsche was contemptuous of those who wanted a firm ground on which to stand. Those who wanted to rely on anything outside themselves showed, he thought, how weak they were. They wanted someone or something else to lean on and guide them, because they themselves 'do not know how to command'. This view of religion as a crutch has gained currency. For Nietzsche, that quest for certainty was linked to fanaticism, the common complaint against religious believers. He defines it as a volitional strength for 'the weak and irresolute', significantly adding that 'the Christian calls it his *faith*'. In contrast, he praises the 'free spirit', who bids 'farewell to every wish for certainty'. He included scientists in the condemnation of those who longed for certainty. Any quest for truth reproduces, it seems, the errors of Christian faith, including that of the rationalism of the 18th-century Enlightenment.

Must certainty and dogmatism be a concomitant of all faith? When any faith becomes too unsure of itself, that may remove its appeal in addressing the doubts and hesitations of wider society. Just because faith is to be distinguished from complete knowledge, there will always be a place for intellectual doubt, and an element of risk in one's commitment. Genuine faith can also be at risk from hesitation, in that we can fail to act, perhaps out of fear, on what we do believe. Some believe that any admission of a lack of knowledge admits a lack of commitment, making any faith seem tentative, lacking the right to speak with authority about the needs of society. Those who speak without conviction, let alone failing to act accordingly, are unlikely to make an impression on others. Listening to opponents could seem like a wavering of allegiance, but a faith that closes minds can become the coercive, fanatical danger to any society that some fear. An unwillingness to face up to external questioning suggests underlying doubt, with less than wholehearted belief in the truth being witnessed to. Criticism need not appear a threat to a person with a deep-rooted faith, which harnesses intellect, will, and emotions. Such calm faith might be a sign of strength, not weakness.

A contemporary Muslim theologian, Shabbir Akhtar, comments: 'No faith or ideology was ever founded on doubt, on acknowledgement of diversity or on the literary apparatus of hesitation that accompanies it. It is intolerant of alternatives. Certainty is a form of authority. In temperament, it is totalitarian, the temper of every successful protest and revolutionary movements.'

The absence of absolute certainty, and a willingness to tolerate others, is made to suggest an imperfect grasp on truth. This fails to appreciate that the nature of divine reality is such that it always transcends our understanding as finite human beings. That could never justify a totalitarian and intolerant attitude but encourages humility in the face of all claims to truth This has major implications for the operation of different faiths within one society, but we have no alternative but to try to live according to such knowledge as we think we have.

Faith must not become a delicate, intellectual game of balancing probabilities, so that it is too detached from genuine commitment. The influential Oxford philosopher of religion Richard Swinburne rightly stresses the intellectual side of faith, but for him, religious belief involves assessing probabilities, based on available evidence. He remarks at the beginning of his book on *Faith and Reason* that 'on balance the various arguments together showed that is more probable than not that there is a God'. Yet few would base their lives on such a detached calculation of probabilities, perhaps even to be formalized in mathematical terms. It is a recurring theme amongst many philosophers of religion that whole-hearted faith is not a mere explanatory hypothesis, nor the product of an intellectual puzzle. It may be a matter of the head but must also engage the heart. It must come to terms with doubt while evoking a whole-hearted commitment that affects the whole of life. When truth is at stake about the most basic questions of human life, no-one can be an interested bystander.

Individuals and the State

John Wesley, the founder of Methodism, preached a powerful sermon 'Salvation by Faith' to the University of Oxford, his own university, in June 1738. He spoke of 'salvation from sin and the consequences of sin'. He spoke of a faith which is 'productive of all good works, and all holiness'. The congregation in the university church would have been composed of academics of the time, who valued cool reason, and distrusted anything approaching 'enthusiasm'. The Church of England, in England and in places such as colonial Virginia, often exhibited then a lifeless and cold rigidity. Not for it was a faith that could change lives, and, as Methodism was later to do, then change society in significant ways.

Wesley's own emphasis on faith fully acknowledged the importance of rational belief. He admired the writings of John Locke, whose influence was pervasive in the 18th century, but Wesley's preaching also challenged individuals to make a full commitment with their whole lives. He did not want any 'cold lifeless assent' but a personal response, leading to action. However important reason, and philosophy itself, may be, it is never the whole of faith. A similar change of heart had occurred in the life of another influential Christian, St Augustine of Hippo. As long ago as the 4th century, he recounts in his *Confessions*, how he was induced to pick up a Bible and open it at random, on hearing a child in a nearby house unusually chanting 'tolle et lege' (take up and read). Augustine was a young but erudite Professor of Rhetoric in Milan, steeped in Greek philosophy, and particularly influenced by Plato. A passage from St Paul's Letter to the Romans, which immediately caught his eye, referred to a person who is 'weak in the faith'. It told him to 'put on' the Lord Jesus Christ, instead of following sensual desires. Augustine realized the gap between his own somewhat dissolute behaviour and what he saw as the holiness of God. His whole life changed, with immense repercussions for the history of Christian thought.

Because of the power of religious faith to influence lives and society in this way, it must be strongly guided by reason. The heart's response can be highly motivating, but it must beware of responding to evil masquerading as truth. The perversion of any religion so that it can inspire cruelty and even terrorism shows how reason and religion are separated at a cost to all society. Evil festers in the shadows when not publicly called to account.

Many have thought society itself can be changed through changing individuals. People must work together in society, but they bring personal experiences and beliefs to bear on what is done collectively. That is an individualist view of society, in contrast to the Marxist view that people are wholly formed by the social and economic structures they inhabit. The latter means that changing individuals involves first changing the nature of society, by revolution if necessary. Individual religious faith can then be seen as inhibiting social progress, and not one of its drivers. Individuals and social structures, however, can each play a part. The role of revolutionary leaders, and the influence of small groups of revolutionaries within a wider society, demonstrates how crucial personal belief and burning faith in some cause, even a secular one, can be. Violent revolutions are led by charismatic individuals whose commitment fires others. On the other side, for people of faith together to have an effect, institutions, such as

Churches, are as necessary as are revolutionary political parties for revolutionaries.

A liberal and pluralist society, which only stresses personal autonomy, can ignore the importance of institutions standing as buffers between individual and State. Individuals resent the constraints, and disciplines, required by membership of Churches and other social organizations. Belonging to any community can come to appear an obstacle to personal fulfilment. Without, however, vibrant institutions giving moral guidance and teaching, everything relies on government policy and the authority of a State. When religious faith is confined to the province of the individual, only a government is left as a source of discipline. 'Society' comes to mean 'the government', and not the myriad intermediate structures from the family to religious communities, trade unions, schools, and the many voluntary groupings of the civic world. The authority of all such bodies decays in the pursuit of the chimera of individual freedom. When the individual is seen as an isolated atom without any social bonds, the State steps in with all its authority, as the only guardian of communal interest.

The separation of Church and State, much alluded to in the United States, was intended to procure important spheres for each. In a secular society, that can come to mean the marginalization of what ecclesiastical and general religious influence is left. The State then functions in total independence and freedom from any idea of faith, the ideal of every totalitarian government. The corollary is that the State does not interfere in what ought to be the province of religious institutions, least of all their doctrines. The practice of any faith should not be at the mercy of politics, or even the will of the people, however much a rigorous secularist approach might suggest otherwise.

Much modern political theory, even if it advocates forms of liberalism, can give a central role to the State. Cecile Laborde, an

Oxford political theorist, thinks that States, not Churches, should determine the extent of their own authority, and the extent of their competence. That, indeed, is inevitable, given a secular view, allowing no role for accountability to any divine authority. The 'secular, democratic state', she maintains, is the arbiter 'of the boundary between public and private'. Any manifestation of faith will then be at the mercy of what the State will and will not allow. She asserts that 'states define what constitutes *harmful* behaviour—a key notion in the regulation of religion, as it sets out the boundary of permissible religious activities'. No corporate body below the level of the State is left to teach about what is harmful. The emphasis on the individual, the mark of liberal philosophy, has an origin in religious views about individual freedom. Then it privatizes faith, so that it appears irrelevant to wider society. The neutrality towards all religions, favoured by such an outlook, entails that religious institutions are not seen as special or as contributing anything of importance to the common life of citizens. That looks like a judgement about faith, not neutrality towards it.

Conclusion

The foundations of democratic society are insecure when constituted by the fleeting opinions of a temporary majority. All nations must have some agreed basis for their citizens' life together for the sake of social cohesion. Different views of human life, some stemming from religious faith, come to varying conclusions about the nature of human flourishing. The United Nations Human Rights Committee in 1993 recognized that 'the concept of morals derives from many social, philosophical and religious traditions'. It concluded that measures to protect morals must be based on 'principles not deriving exclusively from a single tradition'. That however draws attention to a problem without resolving it. Rights and freedoms become the result of political negotiation.

Societies make these problems worse if they exclude different bodies of faith and belief from the public sphere. Because of its central importance in human life, religion can never ultimately be silenced, and should be encouraged to make a positive contribution to society. We live in societies where there is much disagreement, but they all need organizing principles that proclaim what is important in human life. No-one can, in practice, exist in a moral vacuum. Both individually and collectively we all live by beliefs about what we believe to be true. Few can venture knowingly into the abyss of nihilism in which nothing matters except the exercise of power. While every generation must deal with the possibility of nihilism, every religious tradition exists as a riposte to it.

Many despair of finding a collective path to the common good, because of sustained disagreement between different systems of faith within religion and beyond it. They still, however, matter. All face the same world, and all moral beliefs must recognize basic facts of human nature and its needs. When humans are faced with matters beyond their full understanding, they can come to different beliefs and different faiths. The challenge is to organize a society in which all can live together but not be silent about their faith or precluded from putting it into practice. We can listen to those with whom we disagree, even if we remain quietly confident of the truth of our own position. The courage to stand by our beliefs should not be undermined by a necessary humility about our own relative lack of knowledge.

The challenge is to include everyone, of different faiths (and none), within one political community. A distrust of State-enforced orthodoxy must be balanced against the recognition that every State has principles. The pretence of neutrality is hypocritical, unless it ends in paralysis, because any nation lives with an implicit or explicit faith in something. Its citizens must allow that the insights of particular faiths may themselves contribute to the common good. Truth is at stake, even though complete knowledge is beyond our grasp as humans. Every person must live with a faith of some kind, whether they realize it or not. All make some assumptions as starting points.

The idea of faith is multifaceted. Reason is crucial, and alleged tugs between faith and reason will always provoke controversy. Faith, though, is not just a matter of the intellect. Its role in religion has often been regarded as a virtue, even if it needs to be coupled with the virtue of humility. True faith in any area is different from dispassionate detachment and is not the preoccupation of the bystander or spectator. It belongs in the thick of things, bringing full-hearted commitment and action. It demonstrates the kind of person someone is. Faith without works is dead, and private faith without public impact seems contradictory. Genuine faith, whether in a religious belief, a scientific theory, or a political philosophy, eventually involves the whole person, heart and mind.

We cannot be committed to what we recognize as false, but faith involves the will, the imagination, and emotions, as well as the intellect. In Christianity, Catholics have sometimes been said to stress the role of reason, and Protestants the importance of the will. Both are clouded by human limitations and error, but each is involved in any genuine faith. If we think we are recognizing what is true, we should possess the will to act on its demands. Faith can face intellectual doubts, but also be hampered by hesitation. A belief that does not result in appropriate action is empty. Acting without belief is unguided. All faith needs both.

References and further reading

Preface

Hebrews 11:1.

For a more detailed philosophical treatment of some of these themes, see Roger Trigg, *Rationality and Religion: Does Faith need Reason?* Oxford, Wiley/Blackwell, 1998.

For a study by a classical scholar of the notions of faith current at the beginnings of Christianity, see Teresa Morgan, *Roman Faith and Christian Faith: Pistis and Fides in the Early Roman Empire and Early Churches*, Oxford, Oxford University Press, 2015, esp. ch. 1.

Chapter 1: Faith and reason

Jonathan L. Kvanvig, *Faith and Humility*, Oxford, Oxford University Press, 2018, p. 103. The book is a detailed contemporary discussion of philosophical aspects of faith.

There is a large technical literature in recent philosophy of religion on the nature of faith, and its connection with belief, trust, and related concepts. Examples include: D. Howard-Snyder, 'Does Faith Entail Belief?', *Faith and Philosophy*, 33 (2016), pp. 142–62; and essays in a special issue on 'faith' of *International Journal for Philosophy of Religion*, 81 (2017).

See also Robert Audi, *Rationality and Religious Commitment*, Oxford, Oxford University Press, 2011, ch. 3, on faith, belief, and hope.

On various forms of relativism in science, religion, and elsewhere, see Roger Trigg, *Reason and Commitment*, Cambridge, Cambridge

University Press, 1973. For the distinction between reality and human concepts of it, see Roger Trigg, *Reality at Risk*, 2nd edn, London, Simon and Schuster, 1989.

For John Locke on toleration, see his 'A Letter Concerning Toleration' (1688), in *Two Treatises of Government and a Letter Concerning Toleration*, ed. Ian Shapiro, New Haven, Yale University Press, 2003.

A useful collection of Nietzsche's works is *A Nietzsche Reader*, ed. and trans. R. J. Hollingdale, Harmondsworth, Penguin Classics, 1977.

For more on Nietzsche's thought, see Roger Trigg, *Ideas of Human Nature*, 2nd edn, Oxford, Blackwell/Wiley, 1999, ch. 10.

Jean-Luc Marion, *Believing in Order to See*, New York, Fordham University Press, 2017, p. xii.

For Paul Ricoeur on the hermeneutics of suspicion, see *Freud and Philosophy: An Essay in Interpretation*, ed. Denis Savage, New Haven, Yale University Press, 1970, pp. 28ff.

For more on the Cambridge Platonists, see *Cambridge Platonist Spirituality*, ed. Charles Taliaferro and Alison Teply, New York, Paulist Press, 2004.

Karl Barth's major work is *Church Dogmatics*, 4 vols, Edinburgh: T and T Clark, 1962.

For Locke on 'the candle of the Lord', see his *Essay Concerning Human Understanding*, ed. A. S. Pringle Pattison, Oxford, Oxford University Press, 1960, IV, 3, p. 280.

Pope John Paul II, *Fides et Ratio (Faith and Reason)*, Encyclical Letter, London, Catholic Truth Society, 1998.

J. Calvin, *Institutes of the Christian Religion*, esp. book 1, ch. 3—first appearing in 1536 and now available in various editions in English.

Mustafa Akyol, *Reopening Muslim Minds: A Return to Freedom, Reason and Tolerance*, New York, St Martins, 2021, p. 26.

Qu'ran 2, v. 256.

Chapter 2: Faith and God

The classic statement of logical positivism and the verification principle in English was A. J. Ayer, *Language, Truth and Logic*, 2nd edn, London, Victor Gollancz, 1946.

For the role of metaphysics even for empirical science, see Roger Trigg, *Beyond Matter: Why Science Needs Metaphysics*, West Conshohocken, PA, Templeton Press, 2015.

John A. T. Robinson, *Honest to God*, London, SCM Press, 1963, pp. 17 and 29.

Fiona Ellis, *God, Value and Nature*, Oxford, Oxford University Press, 2014, p. 117.

John Dewey, *A Common Faith*, New Haven, Yale University Press, 1960, p. 32.

L. Wittgenstein, *Lectures and Conversations on Aesthetics, Psychology and Religious Belief*, ed. Cyril Barrett, Oxford, Basil Blackwell, 1966, pp. 53ff.

John Cottingham, *Philosophy of Religion*, Cambridge, Cambridge University Press, 2014, p. 16.

S. Kierkegaard, *Concluding Unscientific Postscript*, trans. D. F. Swenson, Princeton, NJ, Princeton University Press, 1941, pp. 216 and 188.

For more on the cognitive science of religion and whether religious belief is natural, see:

Justin Barrett, *Born Believers*, New York, Free Press, 2012.

Roger Trigg and Justin Barrett (eds.), *The Roots of Religion: Exploring the Cognitive Science of Religion*, London, Routledge, 2014.

Claire White, *An Introduction to the Cognitive Science of Religion*, London, Routledge, 2021—a comprehensive textbook.

Chapter 3: Faith and diversity

For more on theism and religious diversity, see Roger Trigg, *Monotheism and Religious Diversity*, Cambridge, Cambridge University Press, 2020.

See also Roger Trigg, 'Diversity and Spiritual Testimony', in *The Testimony of the Spirit: New Essays*, ed. R. Douglas Geivett and Paul K. Moser, New York, Oxford University Press, 2017.

For an introduction to Islamic thought, see Tariq Ramadan, *Islam: The Essentials*, London, Pelican, 2017.

For Locke on revelation, faith, and reason, see his *Essay Concerning Human Understanding*, ed. A. S. Pringle Pattison, Oxford, Oxford University Press, 1960, IV, 19, 4, pp. 355ff.

Richard Hooker, *Of the Laws of Ecclesiastical Polity* (1594), ed. Arthur Stephen McGrade, Oxford, Oxford University Press, 2013 (a modern edition).

For discussions in contemporary philosophy of religion about religious disagreement, see Matthew A. Benton and Jonathan L. Kvanvig

(eds.), *Religious Disagreement and Pluralism*, Oxford, Oxford
University Press, 2021.

Chapter 4: Faith and science

Stephen Pinker, *Enlightenment Now: The Case for Reason, Science,
Humanism and Progress*, London, Allen Lane, 2018, e.g. p. 39. See
also Stephen Pinker, *Rationality*, London, Allen Lane, 2021, p. 70;
also p. 302.

For more on Hume on reason and the passions, see Roger Trigg, *Ideas
of Human Nature*, Oxford, Wiley/Blackwell, 1999, ch. 6.

Brian Leiter, *Why Tolerate Religion?* Princeton, Princeton University
Press, 2013, p. 39.

Jerry Coyne, *Faith versus Facts*, New York, Viking, 2015, pp. 68 and 208.

Romans 1:20.

T. S. Kuhn, *The Structure of Scientific Revolutions*, Chicago, Chicago
University Press, 1962.

For L. Wittgenstein, the duck-rabbit and 'seeing as', see his
Philosophical Investigations, trans. G. E. M. Anscombe, Oxford,
Basil Blackwell, 1958, sect. II xi.

John Hick, *Dialogues in the Philosophy of Religion*, London, Palgrave,
2001, p. 4.

I. Lakatos and A. Musgrave, *Criticism and the Growth of Knowledge*,
Cambridge, Cambridge University Press, 1965, p. 93.

For Wittgenstein on physics and travel to the moon, see his last
notes—published posthumously—*On Certainty*, ed.
G. E. M. Anscombe and G. H. von Wright, Oxford, Blackwell, 1969,
sects. 105ff.—also #209.

For more on Wittgenstein and the nature of concepts—and also the
relationship of the later Wittgenstein to the new cognitive science
of religion—see *Wittgenstein and the Cognitive Science of Religion*,
ed. Robert Vinten, London, Bloomsbury, 2023, an edited collection
of new articles; see particularly Roger Trigg, 'Wittgenstein,
Concepts and Human Nature'.

Chapter 5: Faith and morality

Ephesians 2:8 and 9.

For more on St Thomas Aquinas, see Roger Trigg, *Ideas of Human
Nature*, 2nd edn, Oxford, Wiley/Blackwell, 1999, ch. 3.

Michael Sandel, *The Tyranny of Merit*, London, Allen Lane, 2020, p. 226.

R. B. Braithwaite, 'An Empiricist's View of the Nature of Religious Belief', in *Philosophy of Religion*, ed. Basil Mitchell, Oxford, Oxford University Press, 1971, p. 82.

C. S. Lewis, 'Is Theology Poetry?', *They Asked for a Paper*, London, Geoffrey Bles, 1962, p. 165.

See articles by Frances Young and Denis Nineham in *The Myth of God Incarnate*, ed. John Hick, London, SCM Press, 1977.

For the 'harm principle', see J. S. Mill, 'On Liberty'—a classic available in many editions.

'Dover Beach', a famous lyric poem by Matthew Arnold, was first published in 1867 and is available in many anthologies of poetry.

For Locke on equality, see *Two Treatises of Government and a Letter Concerning Toleration*, 2nd treatise, ed. Ian Shapiro, New Haven, Yale University Press, 2002, p. 102.

Chapter 6: Faith and law

Justice Gorsuch, *Espinoza v. Montana Department of Revenue*; 591_U.S. (2020), 'Concurring Opinion', p. 6.

Brian Leiter: *Why Tolerate Religion?* Princeton, Princeton University Press, 2013, p. 63.

For more on the role of conscience from a secular perspective, see Martha C. Nussbaum, *Liberty of Conscience*, New York, Basic Books, 2008.

For a 'liberal' approach to religion, and a stress on 'individual integrity', see Cecile Laborde, *Liberalism's Religion*, Oxford, Oxford University Press, 2017.

For more on reasonable accommodation in law, see Roger Trigg, *Equality, Freedom and Religion*, Oxford, Oxford University Press, 2012.

For the political relevance of religious diversity, see Roger Trigg, *Religious Diversity: Philosophical and Political Dimensions*, Cambridge, Cambridge University Press, 2015.

Mustafa Akyol, *Islam without Extremes*, New York, W.W. Norton and Company, 2013, p. 46.

Also see Mustafa Akyol, *Reopening Muslim Minds: A Return to Reason, Freedom and Tolerance*, New York, St Martins, 2021.

Shabbir Akhtar, *The New Testament in Muslim Eyes: Paul's Letter to the Galatians*, London, Routledge, 2018, p. 124; also pp. 134 and 30.

Chapter 7: Faith and society

Gianni Vattimo, *A Farewell to Truth*, New York, Columbia University Press, 2011, p. 9; see also p. 71.

For Nietzsche on faith and certainty, see his *The Gay Science*, book 5, sect. 347.

Shabbir Akhtar, *The New Testament in Muslim Eyes*, London, Routledge, 2018, p. 61.

Richard Swinburne, *Faith and Reason*, Oxford, Oxford University Press, 1981.

John Wesley, 'Salvation by Faith', *Forty-Four Sermons*, London, Epworth Press, 1944.

St Augustine, *Confessions*, 8—available in many editions, e.g. London, Penguin Classics, 2002.

Cecile Laborde, *Liberalism's Religion*, Oxford, Oxford University Press, 2017, pp. 165–6.

Faith

Index

For the benefit of digital users, indexed terms that span two pages
(e.g., 52–53) may, on occasion, appear on only one of those pages.

Faith

AGNOSTICISM
A Very Short Introduction
Robin Le Poidevin

What is agnosticism? Is it just the 'don't know' position on God, or is there more to it than this? Is it a belief, or merely the absence of belief? Who were the first to call themselves 'agnostics'? These are just some of the questions that Robin Le Poidevin considers in this *Very Short Introduction*. He sets the philosophical case for agnosticism and explores it as a historical and cultural phenomenon. What emerges is a much more sophisticated, and much more interesting, attitude than a simple failure to either commit to, or reject, religious belief. Le Poidevin challenges some preconceptions and assumptions among both believers and non-atheists, and invites the reader to rethink their own position on the issues.

www.oup.com/vsi

BEAUTY
A Very Short Introduction
Roger Scruton

In this *Very Short Introduction* the renowned philosopher Roger
Scruton explores the concept of beauty, asking what makes an
object - either in art, in nature, or the human form - beautiful,
and examining how we can compare differing judgements of
beauty when it is evident all around us that our tastes vary so
widely. Is there a right judgement to be made about beauty?
Is it right to say there is more beauty in a classical temple than
a concrete office block, more in a Rembrandt than in last year's
Turner Prize winner? Forthright and thought-provoking, and as
accessible as it is intellectually rigorous, this introduction to the
philosophy of beauty draws conclusions that some may find
controversial, but, as Scruton shows, help us to find greater
sense of meaning in the beautiful objects that fill our lives.

A fascinating book, which I heartily recommend.

Brya Wilson, Readers Digest

BIBLICAL ARCHAEOLOGY
A Very Short Introduction
Eric H. Cline

Archaeologist Eric H. Cline here offers a complete overview of this exciting field. He discusses the early pioneers, the origins of biblical archaeology as a discipline, and the major controversies that first prompted explorers to go in search of sites that would "prove" the Bible. He then surveys some of the most well-known modern archaeologists, the sites that are essential sources of knowledge for biblical archaeology, and some of the most important discoveries that have been made in the last half century, including the Dead Sea Scrolls and the Tel Dan Stele.

www.oup.com/vsi

CATHOLICISM
A Very Short Introduction
Gerald O'Collins

Despite a long history of external threats and internal strife, the Roman Catholic Church and the broader reality of Catholicism remain a vast and valuable presence into the third millennium of world history. What are the origins of the Catholic Church? How has Catholicism changed and adapted to such vast and diverse cultural influences over the centuries? What great challenges does the Catholic Church now face in the twenty-first century, both within its own life and in its relation to others around the world? In this Very Short Introduction, Gerald O'Collins draws on the best current scholarship available to answer these questions and to present, in clear and accessible language, a fresh introduction to the largest and oldest institution in the world.

www.oup.com/vsi

CONSCIENCE
A Very Short Introduction
Paul Strohm

In the West conscience has been relied upon for two thousand years as a judgement that distinguishes right from wrong. It has effortlessly moved through every period division and timeline between the ancient, medieval, and modern. The Romans identified it, the early Christians appropriated it, and Reformation Protestants and loyal Catholics relied upon its advice and admonition. Today it is embraced with equal conviction by non-religious and religious alike. Considering its deep historical roots and exploring what it has meant to successive generations, Paul Strohm highlights why this particularly European concept deserves its reputation as 'one of the prouder Western contributions to human rights and human dignity throughout the world.

www.oup.com/vsi

ISLAMIC HISTORY
A Very Short Introduction
Adam J. Silverstein

Does history matter? This book argues not that history matters, but that Islamic history does. This *Very Short Introduction* introduces the story of Islamic history; the controversies surrounding its study; and the significance that it holds - for Muslims and for non-Muslims alike. Opening with a lucid overview of the rise and spread of Islam, from the seventh to twenty first century, the book charts the evolution of what was originally a small, localised community of believers into an international religion with over a billion adherents. Chapters are also dedicated to the peoples - Arabs, Persians, and Turks - who shaped Islamic history, and to three representative institutions - the mosque, jihad, and the caliphate - that highlight Islam's diversity over time.

> 'The book is extremely lucid, readable, sensibly organised, and wears its considerable learning, as they say, 'lightly'.'
>
> BBC History Magazine

LOVE
A Very Short Introduction
Ronald de Sousa

Erotic love has been celebrated in art and poetry as life's most rewarding and exalting experience, worth living and dying for and bringing out the best in ourselves. *And yet it has excused, and even been thought to justify, the most reprehensible crimes. Why should this be?*

This *Very Short Introduction* explores this and other puzzling questions. Ronald de Sousa considers some of the many paradoxes created by love, looking at the different kinds of love (affections, affiliation, *philia*, *storage*, and *agape*) with a focus on *eros*, or romantic love. He considers whether our conventional beliefs about love and sex are deeply irrational and argues that alternative conceptions of love and sex, although hard to formulate and live by, may be worth striving for.

www.oup.com/vsi

PAGANISM
A Very Short Introduction
Owen Davies

This *Very Short Introduction* explores the meaning of paganism - through a chronological overview of the attitudes towards its practices and beliefs - from the ancient world through to the present day. Owen Davies largely looks at paganism through the eyes of the Christian world, and how, over the centuries, notions and representations of its nature were shaped by religious conflict, power struggles, colonialism, and scholarship. Despite the expansion of Christianity and Islam, Pagan cultures continue to exist around the world, whilst in the West new formations of paganism constitute one of the fastest-growing religions.

www.oup.com/vsi